OLD TOWN PLAZA
in
ALBUQUERQUE

OLD TOWN PLAZA
in
ALBUQUERQUE

Debra Montoya

THE
History
PRESS

Published by The History Press
Charleston, SC
www.historypress.com

Opposite: Linda Rambes. *Personal collection by Debra Montoya.*

First published 2023

Manufactured in the United States

ISBN 9781467155090

Library of Congress Control Number: 2023938356

This book is dedicated to my beloved "Nana,"
Linda Rambes-Garcia

CONTENTS

Introduction   9
Old Town Plaza Map   13

1. Old Town Plaza   15
2. San Felipe de Neri Church   28
3. San Felipe de Neri Rectory   37
4. Our Lady of the Angels School   42
5. Sister Blandina Convent   47
6. Jacob Stueckel House   55
7. Herman Blueher House   59
8. Ambrosio Armijo House   64
9. Charles Bottger House   73
10. Cristobal Armijo House   80
11. Manuel Springer House   85
12. Henry Springer Store   90
13. Jesus Romero Store   94
14. El Parrillan   97
15. Jesus Romero House   100
16. Florencio Zamora Store   103
17. Charles Mann Barn and Store   107
18. Antonio Vigil House   110
19. Salvador Armijo House   116
20. Territorial Fair   122

References   129
About the Author   143

INTRODUCTION

San Felipe de Neri Church has served the Catholic community for 317 years, with the first baptism recorded on June 21, 1706. Its mission states, "In the Heart of Albuquerque, we strive to be the heart and hand of God." The beginnings of Albuquerque, New Mexico, as a parish and Old Town Plaza with the rich history and beauty attract thousands of visitors worldwide yearly, and the church should be respected as a place of worship.

The Old Town Plaza site was formally known as El Bosque Grande (the big cottonwood grove) de San Francisco Xavier by the Provisional Viceroy Spanish governor, Don Francisco Cuervo y Valdes, founder of Alburquerque (original spelling) on April 23, 1706. The previous church was originally named San Francisco Xavier for seventy years until Alburquerque was officially founded. The duke later followed orders from the crown that the patron saint was to be changed to San Felipe in honor of King Philip of Spain, and he named the church San Felipe de Neri. Diego de Trujillo owned the first Spanish settlement, El Paraje de las Huertas (place of the orchards). He established the first large hacienda with a farm and orchard before the Pueblo Indian Revolt of 1680 with his wife, children and ranch employees as a small village. The first known Americans to see and visit Albuquerque in March 1807 were Captain Zebulon Pike and his entourage while guests of the Spanish government.

Influential people for the development of Old Town Plaza's existence are Francisco Cuervo y Valdes, who founded Albuquerque; Fray Manuel

Statue of Don Francisco Cuervo y Valdes.
Personal collection by Debra Montoya, 2022.

Moreno, a Franciscan priest; the nineteen original families, including ten soldiers with their women and children from Bernalillo, New Mexico; the Franciscan missionaries; the Jesuits (the Society of Jesus); Jean-Baptiste Lamy, first archbishop; Father Donato Gasparri (superior, business manager); Catholic clergy; Sisters of Loretto; Sisters of Charity; and Sister Blandina Segale. The Armijo family established the first home in the territory in 1706 and were significant to the history in Old Albuquerque as original early settlers who were prominent and respectable in serving the community.

Throughout the late 1800s, Germans, Italians, Irish, French and Spanish families moved to Old Albuquerque. The Rambes, Blueher, Stueckel, Springer, Bottger, Mann and many more families lived in Old Town and married into Spanish families. It was a time when locals spoke numerous languages and built their residences on the plaza. The original architecture of the early residences in the plaza was Queen Anne Italianate style with red brick and white ornate details. This was later hidden from the original beauty when Old Town was modified to become a tourist attraction in the 1950s in Pueblo Revival style. For many years, Old Town was also referred to as *De La Ruca* (of the old). In those days, people referred to themselves by the neighborhoods they lived in, and if you are a historical true Old Towner, that term was used regularly for generations.

In recent years, Brice and Nelda Sewell had a vision to preserve the history and development of Old Town Plaza. They preserved the Casa Armijo (formerly Ambrosio Armijo house, La Placita) while residing there and renting it as apartments. They later opened it as Patio Market with several stores, including Nelda's personal store known as the Crazy Horse Gallery. Her vision along with Father Libertini established the first *farolitos* (luminarias) on display in the plaza every Christmas Eve. This has become a tradition that brings thousands each year.

A special thank-you is due to the Historical Society of New Mexico and Albuquerque Museum for the preservation of the Old Albuquerque history and Father Thomas Steele, SJ, with the church who documented the community and events that affected the parish and people that have been preserved for the history and beginnings of Albuquerque.

Franz Huning (October 1827–November 6, 1905) was a German pioneer and merchant who was influential in the development of Old Albuquerque and the new city of Albuquerque. He arrived in Old Albuquerque in 1852 and worked as a clerk, and in 1857, he opened his own mercantile store with his brother Charles, purchasing wagons and bringing goods from Missouri. He became one of the wealthiest businessmen in the territory, owning a large part of property in Old Town Plaza. He later sold the land and purchased the Hacienda Molino de La Glorieta, expanding and building a flour mill and sawmill. He was president of the Albuquerque publishing company, which issued the first newspaper, the *Albuquerque Daily Journal*. He organized

Huning Castle, circa 1884, on Rail Road Avenue (Central Avenue). *Albuquerque Museum, gift of Historic Albuquerque Inc. PA2019.004.001.*

the first company to manufacture illuminating gas. He was known for selling real estate in the Old Town Plaza and purchasing land when the Atchison, Topeka and Santa Fe Railroad was approaching in 1879–80. The railroad was seeking cheap land for shops and yards, and Huning, Elias S. Stover and William Hazeldine formed the New Mexico Town Company as a subsidiary of the railroad and quietly bought up 3.1 square miles of land. In 1883, Huning built and moved into a house known as Huning Castle, a two-story Italianate mansion with fourteen rooms and a parklike orchard, including a huge aviary and running fountains with swans and lilies enclosed by a white picket fence. His castle had a farm consisting of seven hundred acres, including a family burial plot. It was built to resemble Huning's homeland of Melle, Germany, and was located on Railroad Avenue (Central Avenue and 15th Street). Unfortunately, it was demolished in the 1950s. It was later known as Huning Castle Apartments. Huning's other investments were a hotel and opera house, a street railway, the Albuquerque Gas Company, the *Albuquerque Daily Journal* and the Highland Addition, now the Huning Highland Addition, Albuquerque's first housing subdivision.

What was once known as the Villa de Alburquerque has evolved into a beautiful community that is the heart of the city, touching many lives. It is loved and cherished by the locals and descendants of the early settlers.

OLD TOWN PLAZA MAP

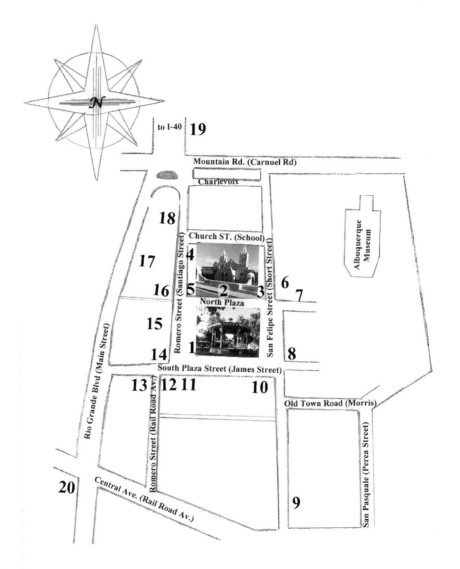

Map Locations, corresponding to the chapters.

Chapter 1

OLD TOWN PLAZA

Nestled in the heart of Albuquerque, New Mexico, lies the historic Old Town Plaza, which receives thousands of locals and tourists yearly. It has an atmosphere of history and is the birthplace of Albuquerque, with a spiritual community for the Catholic Church. It holds enormous pleasant memories for the families of the early settlers with dedication from the community with a rich historic architecture that is fascinating. Before the founding of Alburquerque (spelling changed in 1891) in 1705–6, settlements were established at Bernalillo, Alameda and Atrisco, with Bernalillo making the substantial part of the first Albuquerque population. The first Spanish settlements in Albuquerque were twenty farms along the Rio Grande between Sandia pueblo on the north side and Isleta pueblo on the south side. The first Spanish settlement in Albuquerque was a farm, ranch and orchard named El Paraje de las Huertas (place of the orchards), built by Diego de Trujillo on the site of Old Town in 1632. After Diego's death, the property was left to his wife, Dona Luisa de Trujillo, who was later forced out by the Pueblo Revolt on August 10, 1680. This revolution was against the Spanish religious, economic and political institutions imposed on the Pueblos, who succeeded in overthrowing Spanish rule in New Mexico for twelve years. In 1691, the Spanish crown appointed Diego de Vargas Zapata y Lujan as Spanish governor of the New Spain territory of Santa Fe, New Mexico, to reconquer the territory with an agreement of cooperation and a peaceful promise between both parties. On September 14, 1692, Captain General Diego de Vargas proclaimed a formal

Old Town Plaza, circa 1890. *Albuquerque Museum, gift of Nancy Tucker PA2019.021.050.*

repossession of Albuquerque, returning with settlers and Franciscan priests. They established homes, farms and ranches amid hard times due to a six-year drought, as well as ongoing Apache and Navajo attacks. Unfortunately, Diego de Vargas died in 1704 while on expedition in Bernalillo.

On March 10, 1705, a temporary governor was appointed, Francisco Cuervo y Valdez, from province by the viceroy of New Spain, Francisco Fernandez de la Cueva Enriquez, Duke of Alburquerque. Cuervo was determined to find himself fit for the new assignment and pursued approval from the king of Spain. Upon his early arrival, he was drawn to the area known as El Bosque Grande de Dona Luisa (the large grove of Dona Luisa) near the present Old Town Plaza. This wooded area was named for the widow of Diego de Trujillo, who had built the first estancia in the area in 1632. To make the territory appealing to colonists, Cuervo stationed a detachment of ten soldiers in the area and awarded land grants to settlers. The soldiers who brought families were Captain Don Martin Hurtado, Juan de Pineda, Francisco Garcia, Pedro de Chavez y Duran, Andres de Montoya, Sebastian de Canseco, Antonio de Silva, Jose de Salas, Tomas Garcia and Xavier de Benavides. Additional families settling in Albuquerque were Cristobal Jaramillo, Juan Barela, Francisco Candelaria, Feleciano Candelaria, Nicholas Lucero, Baltazar Romero, Joaquin Sedillo, Antonio Gutierrez, Cristobal Barela, Pedro Lopez y Castillo, Dona Bernardina Sala y Trujillo and Juana Lopez y Castillo. The new establishment was called Villa de Alburquerque and gave as its patron San Francisco Javier.

On April 23, 1706, acting Governor Cuervo notified the king and viceroy that he had founded the Villa de San Francisco de Alburquerque, according to *Works and Days* by Thomas J. Steele and New Mexico State Archives.

> *I, Don Francisco Cuervo y Valdez, Knight of the Order of Santiago, Governor and Captain General of this Kingdom and the province of New Mexico certify to His Majesty (whom may God guard for many years), to his Viceroys, Presidents, Governors and other Officials: That I have founded a Villa on the margin and meadows of the River of the North in a place of good fields, waters, pastures, and timber, distant from this Villa of Santa Fe about twenty-two leagues, giving to it as Patron the most glorious Apostle of the Indies San Francisco Xavier, calling it and naming it the Villa of Alburquerque. There are thirty-five families located there, comprising 252 person, adults, and children. The Church has been completed, capacious and appropriate, with part of the dwelling for the Religious Minister, the government buildings have been begun, and other houses of the settlers are finished with their corrals, irrigation ditches running, fields sowed, all without any expense to the Royal Treasury.*

Cuervo also asked the viceroy, the Duke of Alburquerque for whom he named the settlement, to provide "bells, ornaments, chalices, missals, images, and jewels" with which to furnish the new church. Cuervo had established the villa without consulting or receiving permission from his superiors to obtain a land grant for the villa.

A dissatisfied viceroy wrote back to the acting governor Cuervo in July 1706:

> *On the fourth point in which the said Governor refers to…having founded a Villa which he called Alburquerque, and that it has no bell, altar furniture, chalice nor vessels: It was unanimously resolved that as it is already founded it shall be aided as a favor and that there shall be sent to it on the first opportunity the bell, altar furniture, chalice and vessels as asked for, this assignment being in accordance with the royal law for new settlements, and he being ordered not to make others without informing his Excellency and consulting with him in regard to his reason for the same, in order that he may send him orders as to what he shall do. His Excellency adding that as he has a royal order that a Villa shall be founded with the name of San*

Felipe in memory of his Royal Majesty. The said governor is ordered to call it so for the future and that his resolution be recorded in the archives of the Villa of Santa Fe.

The viceroy proceeded with an order to rename the villa in honor of his superior, Felipe V, king of Spain. Although this did not happen, the name of the patron saint was changed from San Francisco Xavier to San Felipe. The viceroy also regretfully informed Cuervo that the king had appointed José Chacón Medina Salazar y Villaseñor as permanent governor of New Mexico, with Cuervo recalled to Mexico City for other duties. Under the administration of Governor Chacón, several discrepancies were found in the claims of Cuervo regarding the Villa de Alburquerque. In 1712, the viceroy ordered an official inquiry, with Cuervo stating 252 persons were present in the founding of the villa and that a church and government buildings and a proper plaza and streets had been laid out. The transcript revealed a different picture with nineteen original families, including women and children, and 10 soldiers. The nineteen families consisted of 103 people, not counting the dependents of the soldiers, totaling 129 people. The commission of inquiry found that Cuervo had provided land and pre–Pueblo Revolt houses with abandoned existing farms to colonists who came in small groups from settlements in Bernalillo. The church was simple with no plaza, and government buildings did not exist. At the close of the inquiry, the viceroy sanctioned Alburquerque as a villa, with the benefits as an administrative seat in the fertile Rio Abajo (Rio Grande). He also ordered the name be changed to the Villa de Alburquerque de San Felipe de Neri, in honor of Saint Philip, the patron saint of King Philip V of Spain. No charges were brought against the former acting governor Francisco Cuervo y Valdez.

The Villa de Alburquerque de San Felipe de Neri continued with the settlement activity with a farming and ranching community using irrigation from the Rio Grande that drew water from *acequias* (ditches). The original church was known as San Francisco Xavier (1706–92) and had a rectory and corrals with its entrance facing east to the main square of the plaza. It was later rebuilt on the north side of the plaza in 1793 as San Felipe de Neri Church with thick adobe walls as a form of protection from Apache raids. The first recorded home was the Armijo Casa, east of the plaza. It was built in Plazuela style (placita), shaped in a rectangular arrangement of rooms around a courtyard, with a high wall corral covered and gated as a passageway to enter on horseback and wagon. It was built for defense from nomadic

Native Americans. In 1779, the provincial governor ordered Alburquerque's consolidation into a fortified plaza to resist raids by Apache, Navajo and Comanche Native Americans. In 1821, Mexico won independence from Spain. Under Mexican control, New Mexico was allowed to trade with the United States, which led to opening of the Santa Fe Trail. A flag of the Mexican Republic was raised over the plaza as trading began, with wagons crossing through Old Albuquerque on their way to Chihuahua, Mexico. They brought a variety of goods, including new building materials to add and build new homes with accents of Italianate Queen Anne, Gothic and Greek Revival styles, including whitewashed lumber, squared posts, molding capitals, dentils and pitched and gabled roofs.

In 1846, General Stephen Watts Kearney entered Albuquerque and claimed it for the United States, with the army setting up a supply depot west of the plaza and army quarters east of the plaza on former property grounds before the former La Hacienda restaurant. An adobe guardhouse was in the center of the plaza for criminals with a 121-foot-tall flagpole at its center. It was erected at the order of post commander General James Carleton with a Stars and Stripes flag raised over the plaza by the United States troops. In 1848, the Treaty of Guadalupe Hidalgo ended the Mexican-American War, and New Mexico was added to the United States as a territory in 1851.

During the Civil War, on March 2, 1862, the Union cavalry commanded by Captain Herbert M. Enos abandoned the garrison in Albuquerque, burning buildings, food and material and retreating to Fort Union. General Henry Sibley arrived in Old Albuquerque and raised the Confederate flag over the plaza, and Union general E.R.S. Canby began the bombardment of Albuquerque on April 10, 1862. After several hours, he ordered a ceasefire to protect citizens. He was worried a larger group of Sibley's forces would return, and as he only had food for fifteen days and thirty-five to forty rounds of ammunition per man, he quietly moved south during the night. Eight brass howitzer cannons were left behind, buried at a corral behind San Felipe de Neri Church. Two have been preserved at the Albuquerque Museum, with two replicas on display in the center of the plaza.

After the Civil War and under four flags, Old Albuquerque was a supply center. The plaza grounds were open, with only a few cottonwood trees and little landscaping, with bare earth often filled with mud puddles due to flooding. On the north side stood the present-day church with the Gothic twin towers standing twenty feet tall and in Spanish adobe style, including a two-door entry on the west and east sides instead of the front door that exists today. The Campo Santo cemetery originally extended to the front of the 1706 church, estimated sixty feet to the west; in 1868, an eight-foot adobe wall with two carpenter Gothic gates enclosed the cemetery. The rectory at the time was a single-story building open to the plaza, extending east of the church, with the westernmost room as the sacristy that gave access to the church. Behind the rectory and east and north of the church lay the remainder of the original eighteenth-century plaza, which the Jesuits called the Plazuela (little plaza). This became the schoolyard for Our Lady of the Angels, the first public school, and rectory grounds, except for a strip left for a thoroughfare, now named Church Street.

Business around the plaza flourished with eleven mercantile stores, a drugstore, two bakeries, three butchers, one saloon, a carpenter shop, three blacksmiths, a watchmaker, a tailor (Jacob Rambes), a barber, two cobblers and two hotels. On April 17, 1851, New Mexico became a territory of the United States, and on January 6, 1912, it was admitted as the forty-seventh state. A post office officially opened in Old Albuquerque on the plaza, with John Webber as the first postmaster. On December 7, 1867, Melchior Werner was announced as postmaster in the *Albuquerque Weekly Press*. The post office was located in an adobe building on Main Street (Rio Grande) on the west side of the street in the same building as the Centennial Hotel, which Werner also managed. Through the years, many other postmasters existed and operated out of various locations located in the old Sister Blandina Convent and the Charles Mann Store (former Basket Shop). The second and first to New Albuquerque opened on February 10, 1881, when the U.S government issued a charter to F.H. Kent as the postmaster with Bernard Ruppe as his assistant. It was located on Third Street in the Barelas neighborhood. The first original post office in Old Albuquerque remained in operation until a year later, when a postal inspector made the decision to close the Old Albuquerque location, causing an issue with the residents, who claimed they were treated as second-class citizens in favor of citizens of New Town. The U.S Postal Service reopened the original post office on the plaza and designated it as "Armijo," with New Town as "Albuquerque." In 1886, the post office officials changed the name of the Old Town Plaza post office to "Old Albuquerque" and the New Town station as "New Albuquerque." Today, the U.S. Post Office is still in operation in Old Town Plaza on first floor of the Don Luis Plaza.

In 1880, the Atchison, Topeka and Santa Fe Railroad arrived, and development shifted to New Albuquerque near the railroad tracks. Original settlers began selling their property. Sister Blandina Segale "predicted that

San Felipe de Neri Church and Old Town Street Railway, circa 1900. *Albuquerque Museum, gift of Scytha Motto PA1978.077.022.*

Old Town would no longer remain the metropolis with new homes springing up like mushrooms in New Town Albuquerque."

As New Town grew and flourished, Old Town slowly diminished into a neighborhood with new structures appearing on the west and east sides of the plaza combining Adobe with Greek Revival and Queen Anne details. As Albuquerque had become two towns, the Albuquerque Street Railroad incorporated in May 1880, with roads built during the spring of 1881. On May 15, 1881, the first horse-drawn streetcar line was intended to become New Mexico's first mass transit system. The street railroad carried passengers from the corner of First Street and Railroad Avenue (Central Avenue) in New Town, including the Atlantic and Pacific shops, to the plaza heading east on South Plaza (James Street) for a length of three miles and eight cars that made transportation a convenience to the citizens for the cost of a dime.

In 1912, New Mexico was admitted to the Union as the forty-seventh state. The city of Albuquerque annexed Old Town, joining the two officially in 1949. In the 1950s, Old Town Plaza was modified for the "Puebloization" of Old Town as a tourist destination, altering structures as Pueblo Revival architecture. This required the beauty of the Queen Anne Italianate buildings of red brick to be covered with stucco to look like adobe. The Queen Anne–style porches were taken down and instead roughhewn vigas and beams were added, and the pitched roofs were flattened to look pueblo. Old Town Plaza is still the most visited destination in the state of New Mexico as an eighteenth-century Spanish colonial village, with the San Felipe de Neri Church as the focal point of the plaza and its courtyard of green grass, trees and flowers with meticulous attention to detail.

The quaint round gazebo with wood trim and exterior black lantern lights was formerly dominated by a huge flagpole, 121 feet tall, which had been erected by the army shortly before they decamped in 1867. It remained in the plaza with a guardroom at its base and was taken down in 1900, thirty-three years after the military left town. The old solid iron cellblock dating back to 1874 was moved as a jail to the corner of Railroad (Central Avenue) and Main Street (Rio Grande). It served Bernalillo County until 1925, when it was relocated to New Town Albuquerque. The 1874 jail was 20 feet long, with each cell 7 feet high with width and length of 5 feet. In the 1930s, a Works Progress Administration project hired workers to build a stone wall and gazebo. Citizens disapproved of the finished work, deeming it not attractive. The Albuquerque Historical Society did not approve as well and worked for approval for it to be demolished. The plaza grounds have remained open with grass, trees, flowers and intricate antique iron benches surrounded by the rich architecture that reflects the history of Old Albuquerque. According to Sanborn Insurance maps, the streets that surrounded the plaza were named Santiago (Romero), Short (San Felipe) and James (South Plaza), with main streets named Railroad (Central) and Main (Rio Grande).

The annual fiesta of San Felipe de Neri Church dates to the founding of Albuquerque in 1706. The community participates to host the event of history and culture yearly on the first weekend in June. The early settlers attended from such faraway locales as Bernalillo, Peralta, Tome and Tijeras, with visitors staying from the first Friday evening until Monday, when they would begin their trip back home. The early fiestas begin with a solemn mass and procession, including municipal bands and floats carrying parish organizations, banners, city officials, church administration and participants. The plaza provided entertainment with music and traditional New Mexican foods, with children involved in various games such as chasing a greased pig and climbing a greased flagpole. In 1874, the San Felipe de Neri fiesta was memorable because it coincided with the height of the most serious flooding. During the fiesta of 1887, two cannons were discharged on the plaza, but the greatest spectacle of the day was the ascent of two *globos aerostáticos*, some of the earliest hot air balloons in the territory. Today, the fiestas are celebrated as big as the beginnings of the first church with the traditional mass ceremony, procession, religious services and the coronation of a fiesta queen and royal court, including a ball. An entertainment schedule is released for the three-day event, including New Mexico band legends and performers of the traditional flamenco in the center gazebo in the plaza. The plaza is surrounded with food booths from participation of the parish community while the west side of Romero Street is filled with carnival rides and games for the children. The Old Town Plaza fiesta is the first to kick off the summer, and other Catholic parishes follow.

Another huge yearly event is the lighting of the Christmas tree in Don Luis Plaza and the luminarias glowing on Christmas Eve for Holy Night, lining the streets, sidewalks, driveways and rooftops in the historic plaza. This event attracts thousands of people who visit the grounds to see the spectacular view burning all night. The traditionally named *farolitos* (little lights) consist of folded brown paper bags filled with sand and burning candles. It is a custom on Christmas Eve that began during the days of the Spanish colonization of New Mexico. The colonists improvised and made little bonfires of bright burning piñon that created little fires on Christmas Eve, lighting the route of the processions to the village church for midnight mass. They were also placed on the pathways in front of homes so baby Jesus could find his way. Nelda Sewell, owner of Casa Armijo, is responsible for the beginning of the tradition with the thought of spreading the light. In 1950, she and Father Libertini put luminarias all over the plaza, lighting every single candle themselves. As the years

Aerial of Old Town, circa 1955. *Albuquerque Museum, gift of Moriarty Historical Museum PA2000.004.004.*

Old Town on Christmas Eve, circa 1980. *Albuquerque Museum, gift of Steve Donahue PA2000.025.035.*

have passed, the Old Town Merchants Association now pays to have them completed on Christmas Eve day, with candle lighting at dusk. It has become so popular that luminaria bus tours with spectators are sold out within minutes when they go on sale. A traditional midnight mass is held in the San Felipe de Neri Church at full capacity.

As the railroad came through in 1880, Old Town gradually lost the focal point of Old Albuquerque, and they became two towns separated with space and style. They were not united until 1949, when Old Town was formally annexed to the city of Albuquerque. On April 26, 2004, for the Tri-Centennial Celebration, Mayor Martin Chavez had a memorial plaque installed on a lamppost in Old Town Plaza honoring Francisco Cuervo y Valdez as the official founder of the Villa de Alburquerque and Diego Trujillo as the first landowner contributing to Old and New Town Albuquerque.

Today, the plaza remains an atmosphere that attracts people from all over the world. The Albuquerque International Balloon Fiesta is a yearly event that takes place in early October and originated in 1972. It is a nine-day event with more than six hundred balloons each year. It is the largest balloon festival in the world, attracting tourists and locals to visit Old Town Plaza for the rich history; place of worship; architectural history; New Mexican

Old Town Plaza, car enthusiasts Ivan Montoya (Rambes). *Personal collection by Debra Montoya, 2022.*

cuisine famous for the red or green chili; New Mexican merchants with traditional one-of-a-kind items such as Native American jewelry, clothing, leather shoes and belts; and live entertainment with New Mexico band legends. Currently, it also attracts local retired classic car enthusiasts who display their automobiles on the plaza—such as Ivan Montoya (Rambes), Gene Valdez, Joe Gabaldon, Gabe Trujillo, Eddie Torres, Isidoro Garcia, John Klunczyk, Thom Majzun, T. Rock, Ronald Garcia, Philip Chavez and Joseph Paiz—with a deep love and commitment to the parish in a manner of respect to the church and people.

Chapter 2

SAN FELIPE DE NERI CHURCH

2005 North Plaza NW

The original church in the territory was named San Francisco Xavier and had a wooden statue to the patron saint San Francisco Javier in the statuary built by Andras Garcia, parish priest and a Franciscan father. Diego de Vargas Zapata y Lujan Ponce de Leon y Contreras, known as Don Diego de Vargas, was Spanish governor of the New Spain territory of Santa Fe de Nuevo Mexico (1690–95, 1692–96 and 1703–4). He is known for leading the re-conquest of the territory in 1692 following the Pueblo Revolt of 1680 and is commemorated annually during the Fiestas de Santa Fe, New Mexico. He was appointed by the Spanish king to resettle New Mexico with descendants of the first Spanish settlers of 1598 led by Juan Perez de Oñate, first colonial governor, and is credited with the founding of the Province of Santa Fe de Nuevo Mexico. He acted from 1598 to 1610 with an objective to spread Catholicism by establishing new missions in New Mexico. Unfortunately, while on expedition against the Apaches who were plundering in the province, Governor Diego de Vargas became ill and died in Bernalillo in 1704. On March 10, 1705, Francisco Cuervo y Valdés, who had been governor of Nuevo Leon and Coahuila, was chosen as acting governor to New Mexico. He founded the city of Alburquerque (Albuquerque). The church was originally named San Francisco Xavier by Francisco Cuervo y Valdés. The Duke of Alburquerque later ordered that the titular saint be changed to San Felipe de Neri in honor of King Philip V of Spain. The San Felipe de Neri Church started in 1706 under the direction of Fray Manuel Moreno, Franciscan missionary.

San Felipe de Neri Church, circa 1874. *Albuquerque Museum, museum purchase PA2006-011.001.*

The first church was built on the west side of the plaza, with its entrance facing east to the main square. It has been described as a single-nave church, with thick adobe walls, exposed roof beams and an earthen floor. The walled cemetery (Campo Santo) was east of the church, and the convento (rectory) with corral was to the south. Fray Francisco Atanasio Domínguez inspected it in 1776 and wrote the following description in *Works and Days* by Thomas J. Steele:

> The *"first parochial church"* (1706–1792) stood on the west side of the original plaza so that the rising sun would shine through a window over the intersection of nave and sanctuary, lighting the reredos and altar during the hour of mass. The cemetery (campo santo) lay to the north and east of the building, with the rectory for the priest on the south including the corral.
>
> The church is adobe with very thick walls, single-naved, with the outlook and main door to the east. From the door to the ascent to the sanctuary it measures 32 varas long (about 88 feet), 7½ wide (about 21 feet), and the

same height. The roof of the nave consists of 39 beams, and the clerestory rests all along the one that faces the sanctuary. There are ten more in the sanctuary. These, like the others, are wrought and corbeled. The main door has two paneled leaves with a good lock. It is more than 3 varas high (about 8 feet) by 2½ wide (about 7 feet). There is a small arch above this door, containing two middle sized bells (one smaller than the other) which the King gave, and they are now broken. The cemetery is enclosed by a high adobe wall, which has three gates.

The old church was in desperate need of repairs and required constant maintenance. After the rainy summer of 1792, it collapsed at the end of the same year. Governor Fernando de la Concha called the collapse a disgrace and ordered a replacement and all to aid in rebuilding as soon as possible. The new church was built by converted Native Americans from Valencia and Tome working under the direction of Franciscan friars. It was erected in 1793 on the present location of the northern half of the plaza grounds, taking over portions of Campo Santo cemetery. It was built with exterior twin bell towers on the rooftop and the interior designed in a cruciform plan, with a single nave and two intersecting transepts forming the shape of cross. It had a choir loft at the entrance and a projecting apse lit by a transverse clerestory at the end of the nave. The thick adobe walls were supported by vigas on corbel brackets, and it had two large belfries and a simple one-story convento (rectory) built of adobe to the east of the church, with the westernmost room serving as a sacristy room for the Franciscan friars who ran the parish.

Years later, the church was an independent parish with Albuquerque as one of three Spanish towns. The Franciscan friars lived in pueblos and visited Spanish chapels or missions. In 1817, the administration of San Felipe de Neri was transferred to the Diocese of Durango, as the Franciscans had outlived their missionary role and were draining funds as an incentive of support. Jean-Baptiste Lamy—born in Lempdes, Puy-de-Dôme, in the Auvergne region of France, on October 11, 1814—was serving as a missionary in North America with missions in Ohio and Kentucky when he was notified of Pope Pius IX appointing him as bishop of the recently created Apostolic Vicariate of New Mexico on July 23, 1850. Shortly after, he was appointed titular bishop of Agathonice and consecrated a bishop on November 24, 1850. After a long journey, he reached Santa Fe, New Mexico, on August 9, 1851, and was welcomed by Governor James S, Calhoun and other citizens in the territory. However, he was not welcomed by all and was told that local clergy did not recognize his authority, but he continued to remain loyal. On July 23, 1853, the Vicariate of New Mexico was raised to the Diocese of Santa Fe, and Lamy was appointed first bishop. He participated in the First Vatican Council from 1869 to 1870 and was responsible for the construction of the Cathedral Basilica of Saint Francis of Assisi (known as St. Francis Cathedral) and Loretto Chapel in Santa Fe. Lamy ended his tenure as bishop when he resigned in 1885. He passed away on February 13, 1888, at the age of seventy-three in Santa Fe.

His early efforts as bishop were directed to reforming the New Mexico churches, the building and creation of new churches in the territory and the establishment of schools. He was chosen to integrate New Mexican Catholicism into the United States, taking over and supporting the church and the community until the arrival of the Jesuits. Prior to the arrival of the Jesuits between 1817 and 1852, secular (diocesan) priests served San Felipe de Neri Church, with Father Jose Manuel Gallegos serving the parish and the community until a disagreement between Lamy and Gallegos about a "a very handsome lady, who graced the establishment" occurred in 1852. The prelate sent Father Joseph Machebeuf to expel the erring priest over the objections. Gallegos then started a new career in politics in 1853 and was elected territorial delegate to Congress. Bishop Lamy purchased the church, rectory and property from Father Jose Manuel Gallegos (once owned by Jesusa Trujillo, the "very handsome lady" previously mentioned) for $1,000. All church property would belong to the resident clergyman or his order and soon to the Jesuits. During this time, the San Felipe de Neri Church was remodeled with a new roof, altar and pulpit.

The Society of Jesus (the Jesuit order) is a worldwide religious community of priests and brothers within the Catholic Church, and it arrived in Old Albuquerque in 1868. Since its founding in 1540 by St. Ignatius Loyola, it has been organized into provinces and missions under the direction of a regional superior and under the worldwide direction of a superior general in Rome who owes allegiance to the pope. To conduct Bishop Lamy's mission, he needed clergy. He contacted Francesco Ferrante, religious superior of the Dispersed Jesuit Province of Naples in Rome, begging for aid for the work of the church in New Mexico and began assigning men in Spain, Italy and the United States. At the time, Jesuits stationed in Bernalillo tended to Spanish towns and three language groups of the Pueblo Native Americans: the Towa (Jemez), Tiwa (Sandia) and Keres (Zia, Santa Ana, San Felipe, Santo Domingo and Cochiti). While Bishop Lamy fulfilled his promise to give the Jesuits San Felipe de Neri Church and property, there was later confusion on the ownership of the rectory property still belonging to the estate of Jesusa Trujillo. While Father Augustine Truchard returned to occupy the rectory and had previously bought ownership of the property, he was willing to vacate in favor of the Jesuits if they would buy a farm he owned southeast of the plaza (Cerco House), take over his debts and take care of everything while he took a six-month vacation. The Jesuits' acceptance was not for temporal goods but for the sake of the salvation of souls.

At the invitation of Bishop Lamy, orders began with Father Livio Vigilante, the oldest serving priest at fifty-seven years old. He would be superior of the Jesuits. The others attending were Father Raffaele Bianchi, SJ; Brother Prisco Caso, SJ, from Naples; a cook and gardener, Brother Raffaele Vezza, SJ; and Father Donato Maria Gasparri, SJ, born in 1834 in Biscari, Italy, and formerly of Bernalillo and attending priest for the Pueblo of Sandia on May 4, 1868, and later superior, business manager and parish priest in 1870. On November 24, 1868, the title was filed for the possession of the San Felipe de Neri Church, rectory and property to the Jesuits. The Jesuits did not waste any time, and on May 11, 1868, they completed a major facelift to the church, paying a carpenter $18 to build and paint another confessional, since three priests would be available instead of just one. In December 1868, they ordered a new altar, paying $100 for the Santo Entierro, the statue being the buried body of Christ, which lays behind a large pane of glass on one side of the altar. In the sanctuary, at the side of the altar, there was a throne for the bishop costing $6. A history letter of 1872 noted additional church renovations, according to *Works and Days* by Thomas J. Steele:

> *This year also 1868, certain rather major expenditures were made for embellishment of the church, especially the main altar, which had been rather tawdry before it was replaced by a new wooden altar with three arches in front, in the middle one of which a very beautiful statue of the Divine Mother was placed, fashioned of wood and brought from France at a cost of no less than three hundred dollars; this great sum was mostly made up of gifts donated. The other two arches held statues of Saint Joseph and Saint Phillip Neri, patron of the town.*

In 1871, the fathers ordered a large construction project, a series of sacristy rooms along the east wall of the church, with Dona Nieves Sarracino de Armijo, wife of Salvador Armijo, adding the final additions of window curtains. In 1872, needed maintenance of plastering on the church exterior had to be completed for it to survive. The adobe-unfired, sundried mud bricks were laid with mortar and finished with a mud plaster. It was the responsibility of the women called *enjarradores* (potters) to apply the plaster; the task of their husbands' male servants was to mix the adobe plaster for a large job. The religious women of the plaza gathered by appointment for days to complete the challenging work each year before the San Felipe fiesta.

Unfortunately, a mistake was done by the workers, who used straight mud instead of the mixture of mud and straw called *zoguete* (oaf), and two weeks later, it had fallen off and the job had to be redone. The same year, Blas Mata paid ninety dollars to set new front steps from the church down into the new front yard and other necessary work. The church towers got their first coat of hard plaster, a mixture of sand and lime, while Jacobo Moya and Lorenzo Anderson began to paint the towers white reaching to the top of the crosses. The façade of the church got two coats of *yeso* (whitewash). Brother Michael Cofano enlarged the central nicho of the main altar to hold a new and larger statue of San Ignacio donated by the Neapolitan Province. He also put up lamps of tinted glass along the cornice and up and down the pillars of the altar and gave the whole ensemble a new coat of paint. In 1876, the façade was re-plastered numerous times due to a rainstorm, with Jacobo Moya and Pedro Lobato adding new windows in the nave in the sanctuary at either side of the altar and one on the east side of the transept above the door to the sacristy.

The next month, the old floor of the church was torn out and a new wooden one was added, and two years later, a new floor was added at the entry. In November 1876, an American carpenter named Mr. Willey painted one of the pews to serve as a model for the rest. The following year in May 1877, in time for the San Felipe fiesta, American carpenters painted the columns and arches of the church nave and propped up the choir loft with a pair of columns. On June 9, 1877, Brother Cofano finished the two new confessionals, and three days later, Mr. Willey painted the pulpit. In early 1880, a carpenter completed the two side altars. New statues appeared every now and then, including a new statue of the Nuestra Señora de los Dolores, with attire by Father Baldassarre, received on Good Friday 1877 and moved into the sanctuary the following year. Months later, a new door opened at the back of the church nave for easy access to the stairs in the east tower that led to the choir loft with expenses of $3.00 to cut the door, $10.50 for the lumber and $10.75 for the carpenter. At the end of the year, Mr. Willey made the baptismal font, opened one window in the sacristy, replaced two cabinets and transferred a door with a glass window in it from Father Tromby's room to the sacristy. The statue of Mary arrived in 1879, and statues of El Sagrado Corazón and San Jose, which cost $116.55 a pair, were blessed on July 30, 1882. In the spring of 1882, the dirt was removed from the church roof and tin sheets and spouts were installed, replacing the old adobe roof and wooden canals. The new ensemble was painted.

During the next decade, new statues continued to arrive, with the statues of San Felipe and San Francisco Xavier blessed to replace the old ones that had been at the main altar on July 8, 1883. Years later, on March 21, 1887, a heavy wind blew half the tin roof down onto the roof of the convent, leaving it in shreds. The Jesuits not only repaired the roof but also replaced it, adding a low-pitched roof with a stamped tin ceiling. They also started a new series of building projects, including the façade and towers, adding Victorian embellishments in the corbel supports and jig-saw balustrade of the choir loft. By the time the work was completed a year later, they had to sell their Duranes alfalfa farm for $1,000 to cover the expenses.

The book of accounts for the period covers only the church expenditures, including a six-hundred-pound bell bought for $115 from Clinton Meneely of Troy, New York, in August 1891. It was baptized with a full ceremony on August 15, 1891. The Jesuits also paid to add a second story to the rectory with a thirty-foot porch decorated with a gable roof entrance above the front door and a widow's walk on the pitched roof. In 1890, they also built a portico around the courtyard of all the church property.

San Felipe de Neri Church has had minor renovations through the years. In 1916, the interior was painted, a pressed-tin ceiling was added and a new wood floor was installed. In 1950, the exterior Pueblo Revival–style walls wrapping around all the church buildings fronting the plaza were added for the modification during the Puebloization of Old Town as a tourist destination. In 1965, the administration of the church, rectory, Sister Blandina Convent and Our Lady of the Angels School (San Felipe School) returned to the clergy of the Archdiocese of Santa Fe. It was then decided to preserve the building's distinctive mixture of materials and styles. It was originally built with terrones, a packed adobe floor, a flat roof of the earth and a plain exterior. Each phase of construction is an example of the fine architecture for its time in New Mexico, including the massive adobe walls with a single nave, projecting transepts in the shape of a cross, stamped-tin ceiling, twin wood spires standing at each side of the entrance, wood vigas, elaborately carved corbels, polygonal apse, windows, corbel supports and jigsaw balustrade of the choir loft over the gallery main entrance, embellished with Victorian details at the altar of wood painted to look like marble with gold accents and trim. The adorned saints at the altar date

San Felipe de Neri Church. *Personal collection by Debra Montoya, 2022.*

back to the history of the original church. Each feature is remarkable and combines the old and new traditions of New Mexico.

Today, the San Felipe De Neri Church is visible from the plaza, with newer restoration additions completed in three phases in 1996, continuing to 2012 including exterior of the church roof was repaired and refinished.

The interior refurbished with new wood flooring at the altar, brick flooring was added throughout the church, and the two side altars were updated with fresh paint to the altar. The church offices and parish hall were also repaired and remodeled at the same time. The San Felipe De Neri Church is registered as a historic landmark, described as "Spanish Adobe Church" with Gothic trim details from the Historic Landmarks Survey of Albuquerque, NM. It is listed on the National Register of Historic Places on October 1, 1969, and on the State Register of Cultural Properties as part of Old Albuquerque Historic District on February 21, 1969.

San Felipe de Neri Church has continuously served the religious life of the community for 317 years, with the first baptism recorded on June 21, 1706. The parish attracts thousands of tourists yearly with the mission statement "In the Heart of Albuquerque, we strive to be the heart and hand of God." Although it boasts spectacular beauty and historic history, it should be respected as a place of worship.

Chapter 3

SAN FELIPE DE NERI RECTORY

2005 North Plaza NW

T he original rectory adjoining the first church, known as San Francisco Xavier, was built in 1706–92 and stood west of the plaza on the current grounds of Noisy Water Winery (former Old Town Basket Shop and Don Luis Plaza) and south of the church. The rectory originally housed Fray Manuel Moreno, a Franciscan priest, and the Franciscan friars. The original grounds included a cemetery named Campo Santo in 1706, which extended to the front of the original church. The second cemetery was the existing east part of the original Campo Santo; the convent spread in front of the present church and Sister Blandina Convent, which is currently serving as the museum and gift shop. The third cemetery, later moved for the building of the convent, was relocated on Carnuel Road (Mountain Road) north of the Albuquerque Museum and Tiquex Park in 1854–69. This cemetery remained unfenced, open to trespassers and vagrant cows with no graves tended or marked. The land donated by Maria Nieves Sarracino, wife of Salvador Armijo. By 1869, the fourth cemetery was in use at Santa Barbara Calvary, located in Martinez Town (Edith Boulevard NE and Odelia Road NE). With the archbishop's permission, the Jesuits sold the third cemetery property on Carnuel Road, and it currently houses the New Mexico Museum of Natural History and Science, Explora Science Center and Children's Museum of Albuquerque. This section was sold to John Mann, a gardener and truck farmer. He wanted the land for a residence and truck farming garden with the agreement that he would transport any bones that were

San Felipe de Neri Church and rectory, circa 1880. *Albuquerque Museum, gift of Nancy Tucker PA2019.006.022.*

found. As Mann tended to the property for an irrigation system, bones began to appear—hundreds and wagonloads full. According to the *Daily Democrat*, "Pedro Garcia de la Lama and Ochoa who created a display in the window of the newspaper, featuring a child's coffin, its contents, and sundry bones." This created a controversy for the community, which held a protest meeting and sent letters attacking the sale of the cemetery. Unfortunately, there was never any recourse.

The little farm that the Jesuits took over was three acres with a partly constructed house attached to it known as the Cerco House, located at West Mountain Road (Old Town Road) and Perea Street (San Pasquale). As soon as the Jesuits settled into their home in the old rectory, they began to serve the parish and the community. The priests dressed in cassocks, ankle-length, long-sleeved garments of black wool, belted at the waist and worn over trousers and a shirt. By 1870, the Jesuits had to make room for other Jesuits arriving from Europe and had to build an additional living space and buy necessary furniture. By 1872, the Jesuits' Cerco House was debt free, and they extended the house, adding two more living rooms, a wine cellar and a corral for their animals. Their library had also grown, holding 1,400 volumes of every sort of learning. Through the years, they managed to buy land yearly and owned sheep, goats, cows and horses. Sources of income included tithes, gardening and wine vineyards.

Father Donato Gasparri—superior, business manager and parish priest in 1870 and founder of the Jesuit Mission of New Mexico—took his solemn vow as a Jesuit on January 6, 1868, and played a major role in the community of San Felipe de Neri Church and rectory and Our Lady of the Angels School. He reopened a public school and built a school, enclosing the land to the east for a playground, stable and corral. He also built the two-story convent west of the church for the Sisters of Charity in 1881 and convinced them to send six nuns who staffed the parish school and occupied the convent until 1987. This building housed S. Cheryl Ann Grenier, Coletta Marie Kearns and Ann Reimund, among others. Father Donato Gasparri, SJ, was known as an extraordinary man with brilliant intellect and was a walking encyclopedia. He was compassionate, dedicated, polished and charming. He is known as a most noteworthy figure in the history of Old Town Plaza. He died on December 18, 1882, at the age of forty-eight after a painful agony of apoplexy. He was laid to rest beneath the floor of San Felipe de Neri Church adjacent to the sacristy room.

Through the years, the rectory has had many additions to the structure, with the first record in February 1872, which detailed a coat of adobe plaster, an added toilet, a new pantry, a wine cellar, a roof over the portal in the rear and parapets at the top of the walls for water drainage into the back garden. Unfortunately, that same year, the roof leaked due to a rainstorm in late August. In June 1873, the kitchen burned in the middle of the night, causing considerable damage. The community neighbors aided in putting out the flames, and the rebuilding started three weeks later and was completed in six weeks at a cost of $150. The next few years, minor changes were completed, including adding an *horno* (beehive-shaped oven) outside and inside to bake bread and the installation of window and door screens to keep flies out. A major renovation was in place while Luigi Gentile was superior, two years before the construction took place, with actual work beginning in February 1890. The work was completed in fourteen months at a heavy pace employing numerous workers and paying daily wages ranging from $3.00 for lathers, $2.50 for carpenters, $2.00 for bricklayers (with the entire front faced with fired brick) and $0.75 for common laborers. The construction was completed at the end of March 1891 at a cost of $7,000 and incorporated the conveniences of modern life, including a telephone and a recreation room with an in/out board. In a Latin Letter of the house history that is required to be sent to Rome every three years, the San Felipe author for 1889–91 covers the major construction in detail, according to *Works and Days* by Thomas J. Steele:

As soon as Rev. Fr. Capilupi had taken over on 21 September (1889, as superior), he began to build atop this old and humble rectory, adjacent to the east side of the church, another larger and finer structure. To say a bit about it, the façade arises from the old one-story house, over which the second story has been built with an iron roof rising 35 feet from the ground. In the center of the long axis, which is 125 feet, a shorter 30-foot portico extends, supporting a porch at the level of the second story; above this porch and the cornice, a triangular gable rises with a decorative device. There are fourteen rooms, eight bedrooms and the rest for other purposes. Behind the rooms there are two hallways, one above and one below, with two staircases; outside the lower hallway and along the other sides of the house a portico runs around the circle (the inner patio) to give protection from severe weather.

The current rectory started as a simple single-story adobe with three-foot-thick walls and a flat roof. Except for the addition of Territorial-style windows and doors following the annexation of New Mexico as a United States territory in 1848, the structure remained unchanged until the 1880s, when Father Gasparri, SJ, and the Jesuit clergy assumed control of the church. A major renovation took place in 1890, when a second story was added with two-foot-thick adobe brick walls with a low-pitched gable roof with a cross gable marking the front entrance. Below the roof is accented by cornice with brackets in Italianate design. The shingles in the gable are Queen Anne style, with an inset octagonal clock, and all four sides show evidence of windows in all gables. There is a thirty-foot porch with a widow's walk on the pitched roof. Behind the rectory is the parish hall, known as Moreno Hall, named after Fray Manuel Moreno. It was known as a dining hall for the earliest known clergy and was built in the same period, with Territorial windows and details. It is enclosed with two courtyards with flowers, trees and grapevines, as well as a statue of the Virgin Mary. To the east behind the Lady of Angels School and north behind the San Felipe de Neri Church is the Plazuela (small square), which was the enclosed playground, stable and corral, except for a strip for the thoroughfare now named Church Street and parking lot for clergy.

The rectory is registered as a historic landmark with Victorian details with the Historic Landmarks Survey of Albuquerque. It was listed in the National Register of Historic Places as part of San Felipe de Neri Church in 1969 and on the State Register of Cultural Properties as part of Old Albuquerque Historic District in 1979. Today, the rectory is visible from the plaza, with new additions. It was modified during the Puebloization of Old Town in the

San Felipe de Neri rectory. *Personal collection by Debra Montoya, 2022.*

1950s as "Territorial, Italianate and Pueblo Revival." A coat of tan stucco mimicking adobe was applied over the brick facing that had masked the original adobe construction. The wooden portico on the front was replaced by one in the California Mission style, with round arches on large square piers; the rear portico, facing an interior courtyard, was remodeled as a Spanish Colonial Revival portico with corbel bracket capitals set between timber posts and beams. The rectory garden was enclosed by an adobe wall and entrance gate. The rectory was again remodeled in 1995–96 and remains a venerable history asset to San Felipe de Neri Church.

Chapter 4

OUR LADY OF THE ANGELS SCHOOL

320 Romero Street NW (Santiago Street)

The early history of education in New Mexico began in 1599 by the Franciscans who had accompanied Oñate. When the Spaniards were evicted in 1680, the Franciscans could not continue their work until the reconquer of Diego de Vargas Zapata y Luján Ponce de León y Contreras, known as Don Diego de Vargas, Spanish governor of New Spain territory of Santa Fe to the United States and Arizona (1690–95). At that time, the Franciscans used educational methods to teach among the Native Americans, opening avenues to the Spanish children. In 1721, Philip V (Philippe duc d'Anjou), king of Spain, ordered public schools to be established. A law passed in 1823 to establish a high school in El Paso del Norte (Juarez). Two colleges were established in 1826, one in Santa Fe by Vicar General Fernandez and one in Taos, New Mexico, by Padre Martinez, with each paying all expenses on their own with positive results. At the same time, there were seventeen schools scattered in the territory. By 1844, schools were opened in various places by Mariano Martinez de Lejanza, acting Mexican governor of Santa Fe. With his own money, he had two professors come from Europe to keep public schools with military instruction in Santa Fe.

San Felipe de Neri Church in Old Albuquerque, originally under the authority of Bishop of Durango serving secular clergy of that country, came under the United States after the Mexican War in 1848. Jean Baptiste Lamy, archbishop and first bishop of the Diocese of Santa Fe and a native of Claremont, France, served as a priest in the Diocese of Cincinnati, Ohio,

Our Lady of the Angels School, February 1943. *Albuquerque Museum, courtesy of Library of Congress PA1972.154.001.*

from 1839 to 1850. He arrived in New Mexico in 1850 and believed that religious education for children was necessary. He at once set out to establish Spanish-language parochial schools in Old Albuquerque and Santa Fe. Lamy staffed the parochial schools with the services of Sisters of Loretto, Jesuits and Sisters of Charity. The Sisters of Loretto operated the first small school west of San Felipe de Neri Church until they were forced to leave in 1869. Due to government, public interest, Native American conflict and the Civil War, the territorial government was prevented from addressing education until 1872, when counties were authorized to spend public funds on education.

The Jesuits dominated early education in New Mexico under Father Donato Maria Gasparri, superior of the Society of Jesus in New Mexico from 1869 to 1874. He accepted Bishop Lamy's invitation to promote parochial schools in New Mexico. In 1872, Catholics, including priests, were elected to the new county school board. Father Gasparri, with much hesitation, agreed to serve as superintendent of schools for Bernalillo County. Under his direction, a public school named Holy Family Select School for Boys was opened in 1872, run by the Jesuits and supported by public funds. It operated in the building previously used by the Sisters of Loretto but needed repairs due to a flood in 1869, and they were forced to move classes to the home of Ambrosio Armijo in the former Casa Armijo. The Jesuits were paid $600 per school year from November to August to supply free classes for sixty boys. The curriculum consisted of English, arithmetic, geography and writing in Spanish. The school had outgrown the home of Ambrosio Armijo, and plans were in place for construction of a new school building.

Construction began on the former property that housed the Sisters of Loretto schoolhouse. The new construction was a single-story adobe structure measuring eighty-five by twenty-five feet, with cross-gabled roof on entry and a flat roof of earth and a ceiling height of thirteen feet. Constructed on a stone foundation, it consisted of two large classrooms with a flanking entrance hall. The exterior was distinguished with Greek pediment details on the door, windows carved with dentils, volutes and acanthus leaves of the Corinthian capitals that frame the main entrance. The building was topped with a small wooden bell tower. The land to the east was enclosed for a playground, stable and corral.

According to the *Albuquerque Review* of November 23, 1878:

> *Its cost was borne by the Jesuit Fathers of Albuquerque who attended to every detail of its fabrication. Miche McGuire raised the walls and Brother Colano and Mr. Willey of this town, all first-class mechanics, executed the finer woodwork. Pedro Lobato did the roofing and flooring. The roof is flat and covered with earth like all other buildings in New Mexico, but as such roofs are subject to leaks, the Reverend Fathers intend, when able, to replace the present by a lighter one of waterproof material.*

Bainbridge Bunting, an architectural historian, stated, "It contains one of the handsomest Territorial doors in the state. The detail is carved from a single board, not tacked on, while the volutes and acanthus leafs of the capitals carved separately out of three-quarter inch boards and ingeniously fitted together in rough approximation of the Corinthian order."

Construction of Our Lady of the Angels School was completed in 1877, and it was temporarily used as a town hall until classes started in the fall of 1878. The superior of the Jesuits, Reverend Father A.M. Gentile, SJ, and Reverend Father Gasparri, SJ, traveled to Santa Fe in October 1880 to apply to Mother Regina Mattingly to have the Sisters of the Charity open a school in Old Albuquerque. Upon agreement, the Jesuits would build a house for the sisters, furnish it and give them the deed, with the understanding that the sisters were to support themselves. The Jesuits began significant repairs to the schoolhouse, including a new pitched tin roof, before the Sisters' arrival. Mother Regina appointed Sister Blandina to make all preliminary arrangements necessary for both parties. With the arrival of the railroad in 1880, increasing numbers of Protestant families arrived and took steps to establish schools for their children. In 1879, Colorado College of Colorado Springs started Albuquerque Academy, a tuition school (not to be confused with the present institution of the same name) in Old Albuquerque, east of San Felipe de Neri Church, on former military base property in an old adobe structure as a Protestant boarding school. It later moved to New Albuquerque in 1881 and was the beginning of Albuquerque High School. In February 1881, Reverend Donato Gasparri, SJ, wrote to Sister Blandina in Santa Fe at the request of Nieves Armijo, former wife of Salvador Armijo, in Old Albuquerque to request a visit and offer a donation to the Sisters of the Charity. Sister Blandina and Sister Augusta attended at her request, and they were introduced to a lawyer named Werner, surrounded with a stack of papers. He expressed that he was serving at the request of Nieves Armijo to offer the donation of her home, garden and vineyards. The offer did not sit well with the sisters, thinking of the hardship of her daughter, husband and children, and they did not accept the offer.

On August 21, 1881, the General Superiors in Cincinnati, Ohio, and Mother Regina appointed Sisters Mary Josephine Irwin, superior; Blandina Segale, treasurer and music teacher; Pauline Leo; Agnes Cecilia Stanley; Gertrudis Duran; and Mary Alacoque Gallaghan to open the first public school in Albuquerque, known as Our Lady of the Angels, on September 21, 1881. Since the school was public, the town paid the sisters twelve dollars monthly to teach elementary and grammar subjects. Two groups of students attended the school: those who received the general instruction free of charge and those who paid for private lessons in music, art, languages and other requested subjects. On December 10, 1881, in preparation for Christmas, a tree was set up for the Native children who had no knowledge of Santa Claus; Sister Blandina directed the choir presentation of Mozart's Mass for Christmas 1881. On September 4, 1882, Our Lady of the Angels reopened for the second school year as a public day school, offering elementary and grammar subjects, while the adjoining convent offered lessons in music, art, languages and other subjects requested.

In 1960, the building was converted for use as a parish hall and gift shop. The interior was partitioned with a door added to the south, an original

Our Lady of the
Angels School.
*Personal collection by
Debra Montoya, 2022.*

window was replaced and modern stucco was applied to the exterior. In 1962, the Albuquerque Historical Society, a predecessor of the Albuquerque Museum, arranged to lease the former Our Lady of the Angels School building from the parish. In 1963, two classrooms of third and fourth grades at San Jose and Los Duranes closed, and San Felipe School offered the fall classes. In 1964, the extension school closed, and all children attended the main San Felipe School. The school board organized on October 8, 1965, to add aid to the principal and administration of the school. Today, it is operating as Trader Barbs Gallery and is one of the least altered buildings in Old Town. Our Lady of the Angels School is registered as a historic landmark, described as "Territorial Style, with Gothic door molding" in the Historic Landmarks Survey of Albuquerque. It was listed in the State Register of Cultural Properties as part of the Old Albuquerque Historic District in 1979 and in the National Register of Historic Places on November 29, 1984.

Chapter 5

SISTER BLANDINA CONVENT

2005 North Plaza Street NW

The convent was built by Father Donato Gasparri for the agreement of Sisters of Charity to teach at Our Lady of the Angels School and housed the appointed sisters, Mary Josephine Irwin, Blandina Segale, Pauline Leo, Agnes Cecilia Stanley, Gertrudis Duran and Mary Alacoque Gallaghan. Our Lady of the Angels School, formerly taught by the Jesuits and now an Old Town public school, opened on September 21, 1881, under the direction of the Sisters of the Charity. Father Donato Gasparri intended the use of a large eighteen-room house with a plaza and corral in mind for the sisters, but it had an existing lease with Don Nicolas Armijo. He was willing to vacate, but this was impossible until he built another home for his family. Father Gasparri began building the sisters a residence west of the San Felipe de Neri Church on land previously used as Campo Santo cemetery. The bodies had to be exhumed and relocated to Santa Barbara cemetery in the Martinez Town neighborhood in New Albuquerque.

While construction proceeded, so did the rainy season. The construction of the two-story building began in March 1881, with difficulty, and one corner of the house crumbled down. The builders were not familiar with building anything higher than a one-story adobe. The first time the corner collapsed, the workers were excited and confirmed that only a one-story adobe can stand the climate. The workers continued rebuilding, but after the third collapse with no success, Sister Blandina traveled to Santa Fe and arranged for an Italian stonecutter to lay a stone foundation. He carried the stonework halfway above the first story, which improved the building

Cobb Studio, Sister Blandina Convent, 1891. *Albuquerque Museum, museum purchase PA1990.013.134.*

Sister Blandina Convent. *Personal collection by Debra Montoya, 2022.*

progression with no more difficulty. While construction was taking place, the Jesuits asked that the sisters remain in Old Albuquerque a few days to look over necessary preparations.

The new convent completed in 1881 for the Sisters of Charity was a log-raftered, mud-floored adobe built next to San Felipe de Neri Church. Sister Blandina Convent is registered as a historic landmark, described as "Remodeled Convent" by the Historic Landmarks Survey of Albuquerque. It was listed in the State Register of Cultural Properties as part of the Old Albuquerque Historic District in 1979. It served simultaneously as a convent, school, infirmary and U.S. Post Office. Sister Blandina always referred to it as Wayfarers House. The lower level of the convent was converted into five added classrooms to accommodate the increase of students. A passageway connected the convent with Our Lady of the Angels Day School, offering elementary and grammar subjects, with the adjoining convent offering lessons in music, art, languages and other subjects requested. Each teaching sister received a salary of twelve dollars monthly from the town. In the *Albuquerque Morning Journal* for September 1, 1882, appeared the following advertisement:

Our Lady of Angels!
Under the direction of the
Sisters of Charity,
Will re-open
Monday, September 4, 1882
All useful and ornamental branches
Taught. Painting, Drawing, and Wax
Work. Spanish classes and private lessons.
For particulars, apply at the Convent

Sister Blandina had previously predicted with the arrival of the railroad in April 1880 that Old Albuquerque would not remain the metropolis and people would begin building adjacent to the railroad station. She was given charge of a building in New Town (Albuquerque) on Sixth Street and New York Avenue (Lomas) in the Armijo addition (Perfecto, Mariano and Jesus Armijo) with an additional tract of land to the north given to San Felipe de Neri Church. The first wing addition of the new school of Our Lady of the Angels in New Town Albuquerque was completed on January 9, 1884. It was known as Public School Precinct Number Twelve (later becoming St. Vincent Academy). Sister Blandina opened a full academic curriculum, including music, art and modern languages. The subjects taught in both schools were those required by law: writing, spelling, arithmetic, English, Spanish, geography and United States history. The private schools also offered religion, higher arithmetic, philosophy, botany, physiology, Latin, music and drawing.

Old Albuquerque and New Albuquerque were separate schools preparing for future growth. A new wing addition was constructed to the New Town Academy as a boarding school for girls on the same property in 1887, while Our Lady of the Angels and Convent continued to serve as a day school and offered other subjects as requested. During this time, Sister Blandina was working on several other missions in the territory. Her efforts were to help the sick with no hospital, no place to care for abandoned children, no committees to care for the needy and a needed industrial school to teach trades. She made it mandatory to herself to visit the inmates in the jail. She was currently obtaining the previously offered first house with the eighteen rooms from Father Donato that was not available at the time for the Sisters of the Charity.

In May 1883, Sister Blandina was called to respond to the actions of some of the Native American agents who were depriving the Native American tribes of supplies sent by the government. A Native American school was also located in new Albuquerque, with the recent dismissal of the superintendent and teachers. The new superintendent offered a monthly salary to teach Christian doctrine to the pupils. The Sisters of Charity proposed that the Native American pupils could attend on Sundays, and they would open a Sunday school for them, providing teachers for instruction, grade them into classes and would then lead them to church after with no salary. The offer was accepted, with the sisters pleased for the opportunity to teach.

In February 1885, the Sisters of Charity secured sixty-four additional lots in New Albuquerque, realizing that Old Albuquerque would remain status quo and New Albuquerque would soon progress. While Sister Blandina was working on other missions, she was superintending the New Town Academy building and the eighteen-room house used for emergency distress cases. In July 1885, added space was needed for the New Town Academy building with new construction to adjoin to the main structure of the building designed by Jose Apodaca. The addition consisted of adobe and four rooms with a tar and pebble–covered roof and was completed in 1885. On May 9, 1889, the financial debt for New Town Academy was dissolved, with the convent of the Sisters of Charity in Old Albuquerque paying off the financial debt. What remained to be paid was a small amount to Jesus and Mariano Armijo

Bernalillo County Courthouse, circa 1890. *Albuquerque Museum, gift of Diane Gerow PA1973.012.015.*

families with payment in educational terms. Don Perfecto Armijo's children were to attend the academy (boarding school) in Cincinnati, Ohio.

In 1891, the territorial legislature school board asked that the sisters take the public school examination. Sister Blandina agreed on the importance of the exam, with three other sisters completed it. A few days after the examination, Mr. Bond and others from the examination board visited the convent to present their certificates. They personally wanted the pleasure of naming the first four number-one teachers in Old Albuquerque under the new school law. In the summer of 1892, Sister Blandina was called to meet the school board. The meeting was to notify the sisters that if they wanted to continue teaching, they had to change their all-black dress code. Under the new statute declared for public schools, they must be nonsectarian and must speak and teach the English language. Unfortunately, this was the end of the twenty-two years of work beginning with Public School Number One, opened in 1870 in Trinidad, Colorado, for Sister Blandina and the Sisters of Charity.

Our Lady of the Angels School in Old Albuquerque reopened as a private school, but because of a lack of funds in 1894, it closed temporarily. It later reopened on January 1, 1895. With the continued rapid growth of pupils, the five classrooms on the bottom floor of the convent could no longer serve the growing number of students. In 1897, the sisters moved from Old Albuquerque to the New Academy (St. Vincent Academy) in New Albuquerque. The Old Courthouse, built in 1886 at the southeast corner of New York Avenue (Lomas) and Perea Street (San Pasquale), was designed by architect Frank E. Edbrooke as a Richardsonian Romanesque–style building constructed of rusticated sandstone skillfully laid by Italian stonemasons. It was bought for the expansion of Our Lady of the Angels School. The building needed minor renovations, and when completed, it was renamed and housed San Felipe School in September 1927. The third floor was used for an auditorium for plays, programs and meetings. The sisters continued to live at the New Academy in New Albuquerque during this time. The old convent building in Old Albuquerque was used as a U.S Post Office from 1934 to 1945. The sisters commuted by horse and buggy and soon returned to live in their original convent after renovations were completed in 1950. It was later renamed Sister Blandina Convent. The convent closed in 1987 and today is operating as the San Felipe de Neri Gift Shop and Museum.

Throughout the years, significant changes have taken place with the new San Felipe school property grounds and the curriculum. In 1954, Archbishop Edwin V. Byrne granted permission to build a new school on grounds behind the old courthouse school. It was built with four classrooms, an office, a lavatory and a library. In the same year, ninth-grade classes were added to all grade schools. Julia Bottger donated a piece of land from the Bottger estate to build the junior high school, with dedication, procession and blessing of the building on January 29, 1956, by Archbishop Byrne. Father Robert M. Libertini, SJ, purchased property from Charles Ramsay for $2,000 to build an elementary school, gym and cafeteria serving hot lunches for twenty-five cents. The property was located behind the new junior high school building. In 1958, the children attended classes for the last time in the old courthouse building. On Sunday, January 4, 1959, Archbishop Byrne blessed and dedicated the new building, and the next day, four hundred children, five lay teachers and five sisters entered their new school building, with each child carrying their own desk and belongings to resume classes by 11:00 a.m.

On Saturday, June 27, 1959, the old courthouse was demolished after serving as San Felipe School for thirty-one years to make room for a playground for the schoolchildren. During the same time, a new hall and classrooms were built behind the mission of Duranes. Classes were taught as an extension of San Felipe School, also serving the children of Duranes. In 1961, Catechism classes were taught at San Felipe School weekly with 3 sisters and 6 lay teachers serving 158 children. Duranes maintained the same schedule with 3 sisters and 8 lay teachers serving 158 children. In 1963, two classrooms of third and fourth graders at San Jose and Los Duranes were closed, with San Felipe School offering all the classes. In 1964, the extension school closed, and all children began attending the main San Felipe School. The school board organized on October 8, 1965, adding assistance to the principal with the administration of the school. The Sisters of Charity left the Sister Blandina Convent in 1987; the last sisters housed there were S. Cheryl Ann Grenier, Coletta Marie Kearns and Ann Reimund.

Sister Blandina was devoted to her mission and the people in need. Arriving first to Trinidad, Colorado, in 1872, she began teaching the poor and built a one-story public schoolhouse with no funds and with no debt. In 1877, she was transferred to Santa Fe, where she co-founded the Catholic and public schools and initiated construction of a three-story hospital without resources. In 1881, she was transferred to Old Albuquerque, where she established a public school, hospital, orphanage and trade school. She served the sick, the poor and the inmates in jail. She aided the Native Americans for fair treatment from the government and supplied schools to the Native American children. She met outlaws and criminals, including Billy the Kid and his gang, with compassion. Her heroic virtues and her tireless efforts to all in need were given with a mother's love.

SISTER BLANDINA SEGALE

Sister Blandina Segale, circa 1880. *Albuquerque Museum, gift of Center for Southwest Research, University of New Mexico PA1978.050.841.*

In 1897, she founded the Santa Maria Institute in Cincinnati, Ohio, serving immigrants. She led the organization until 1933. In 1900, she returned to Albuquerque for two years to assist with the building of St. Joseph Hospital, serving today as CHI St. Joseph's Children, also known as St. Joseph Community Health. She traveled to Italy at the age of eighty-one to meet with Pope Pius to plead for St. Elizabeth's cause. Sister Blandina, a servant of God, died on February 23, 1941, in Cincinnati at the Mother House of the Sisters of Charity at the age of ninety-one. Her last words were "Gesu e Madre (Jesus and Mother)."

On June 25, 2014, Archbishop Michael J. Sheehan held a joint press conference with CHI St. Joseph's Children to announce the Vatican's immediate permission to open the sainthood cause of servant of God for Sister Blandina Segale, SC. Archbishop Sheehan received permission to open the cause of beatification from the Vatican via the Congregation for the Cause of Saints. Archbishop Sheehan was named judge for the cause; Most Reverend Ricardo Ramirez, bishop emeritus of Las Cruces, was named postulator; and Allen Sanchez, president and CEO of CHI St. Joseph's Children, was designated petitioner. This is the first time in the four-hundred-year history of New Mexico's Roman Catholic Church that a decree opening the cause of beatification and canonization has been declared. On April 26, 2004, for the Tri-Centennial Celebration, Mayor Martin Chavez had a memorial plaque installed on a lamppost in Old Town Plaza, honoring Sister Blandina Segale as an educator and establisher of schools and contributed to both Old and New Town, Albuquerque.

Chapter 6

JACOB STUECKEL HOUSE

306 San Felipe Street NW (Short Street)

Jacob Stueckel was born on November 29, 1864, in Mascoutah, Illinois. He was the son of John and Catarin Stueckel, descendants of Germany. In 1894, Jacob married Margaret, and they had four children. Jacob and family moved to Old Albuquerque in 1889. Jacob's occupation in Mascoutah was a gardener and truck gardener. Upon arrival to Old Albuquerque, he found a job as a foreman for Herman Blueher, Market Garden. Records indicate that he was from the same hometown as Blueher, and they possibly knew each other prior to his arrival in Old Albuquerque. He worked for Blueher for fifteen years and went into the gardening business for himself. He was one of the county's most successful garden truck raisers in Old Albuquerque. In 1896, he rented the vacant Ambrosio Armijo home until he built his new home.

He built a simple square four-room adobe house on the northeast corner of the plaza, north from the Blueher home on Short Street (306 San Felipe Street), in 1897, on land owned by Herman Blueher. The home design was a gingerbread façade with a combination of Victorian and Adobe style. The exterior had a high pitch roof, arched elongated wood trim windows and wood trim door with upper window. The exterior had ornate Queen Anne trim with white corbels attached to the sides of the home and extended outward. The exterior was hand painted by Jacob to look like simulated brick. The interior had a fireplace, hardwood floors and a wine cellar underneath the house to store his barrels of homemade wine.

Left: Stueckel House, circa 1900. *Albuquerque Museum, gift of Center for Southwest Research, University of New Mexico PA1978.050.737.*

Below: Cobb Studio, wine tasting in front of the Stueckel House, with Jacob Stueckel, Edwardo Rambes and Herman Blueher, 1901. *Albuquerque Museum, museum purchase PA1990.013.223.*

Opposite: Stueckel/Rambes House. *Personal collection by Debra Montoya, 2022.*

In 1910, his mother, Catarin, and brother Luie moved to Old Albuquerque to live with Jacob and family after the death of his father, John Stueckel. Jacob sold the home to purchase a larger home in the Duranes neighborhood (north of Old Albuquerque). For years, he continued with the gardening business and was successful until his death on June 25, 1944. Jacob sold the residence to Edwardo Rambes, born on March 11, 1896, the son of Jacob Rambes and Antonia Rambes. Jacob was the only tailor in the territory. His son Edwardo served as a private in the U.S. Army during World War I. After his military service, he returned home to Old Albuquerque, where he worked as a farm laborer with Blueher Market Garden and in later years as a car mechanic. Edwardo Rambes married Teresa Lucero, daughter of Florencio and Cipriana Lucero, on February 1, 1919, at San Felipe de Neri Church. They lived on Short Street (306 San Felipe Street) for twenty years with their children Maunelita (Atocha), Mary, Antonia (Tonia), Merlinda (Linda), Lawrence, Emilio, Joseph, Larry and Max Rambes. The locals knew Edwardo as "El Pinionero" (the Pine Tree) because he sold piñon nuts. I can recall my nana, Linda Rambes-Garcia, saying as a little girl she would sell a shot glass filled with piñon nuts for five cents. The Rambes family later moved to a larger home west of Old Town Plaza on Hollywood Avenue and remained in that home until their deaths.

Today, the home is visible from the plaza, with new additions. It was modified during the Puebloization of Old Town in the 1950s as Territorial style. A new pitched roof was added, along with colored stucco with extending white corbels cut off. The interior is original including fireplace, hardwood floors and some wall cabinets. The trapdoor leading down to the wine cellar is operable with access. The wood trim around the now window-enclosed front porch, the roof trim and the gazebo were salvaged from Victorian houses due to demolition in the 1950s. It is registered as a historic landmark, described as "Territorial Adobe" style by the Historic Landmarks Survey of Albuquerque.

For many years, the Stueckel residence remained a private home until Old Town was re-adapted as a tourist attraction. The Stueckel home has had many owners and businesses through the years. In the early 1950s, it was the Plaza Gallery and sold paintings, sculptures, prints and crafts. In 1954, Mr. and Mrs. Louis Ferster bought the property as their home and opened the Blue Gate Southwestern Fashion Shop. Louis installed a brick patio behind the home and installed the trademark blue gate at the entrance. He also raised lanterns and adobe walls. The home was sold in 1958, and the new owner added the Territorial-style porch to the front of the home. Today, it is Kyra's Arts Imports and La Choco shops.

Chapter 7

HERMAN BLUEHER HOUSE

302 San Felipe Street NW (Short Street)

T he property ground is part of the original Spanish land grant, by decree of King Philip V of Spain in 1706, which established the Villa de Alburquerque (the four-square Spanish leagues from the center of the plaza). The villa was a military base during Old Albuquerque and was under four flags: Spain, Mexico, the Confederate States and the United States of America. The U.S. Army rented the old adobe structure as office quarters with prominent soldiers stationed here, including Colonel Kit Carson, General Nelson Appleton Miles, Major General James Longstreet and General Philip Henry Sheridan, from United States Army and Civil War fame. In 1879, Colorado College of Colorado Springs started Albuquerque Academy (not to be confused with the present Albuquerque Academy, founded in 1955) as a Protestant boarding school on former property grounds in a small adobe structure accommodating two classes that made up a total enrollment of twenty-seven pupils. This was the beginning of what was to become Albuquerque High School.

Herman Blueher was born on June 27, 1862, in Mascoutah, Illinois. He was the son of Heinrich and Catharina Blueher, descendants from Germany. Heinrich immigrated to the United States in 1853, to the state of Illinois. During this time, he married Catharina Franck on March 8, 1857, in St. Clair Township, St. Clair, Illinois, and had five children. Unfortunately, Catharina died on November 10, 1891. After her death, Herman's father, Heinrich, moved to Old Albuquerque to live with his son.

Blueher (*right*) and Stueckel Houses, circa 1900. *Albuquerque Museum, gift of Center for Southwest Research, University of New Mexico PA1978.050.737.*

Blueher Pond, circa 1900. This is the present site of Tiquex Park in Old Town. *Albuquerque Museum, gift of Margaret Owen Porter PA1980.092.007.*

Herman left his home to work as a market gardener in St. Louis, Missouri, in March 1877. He worked for five years, learning all the details of producing and shipping vegetables. In January 1882, he moved to Old Albuquerque with $15 and found work with Reagan & Messick Gardeners. He leased a small piece of land from the prominent Armijo family and began raising vegetables as a market garden; he purchased the land in 1896. Blueher started his market and truck garden on thirty-five acres of a triangular farm known today as Tiquex Park, located at Carnuel Road (Mountain Road) and Morris (Old Town Road). That same year, he joined John Mann, gardener and truck farmer and a former employee of Reagan & Messick Gardeners. Herman also introduced draft horses in the territory, leaving his garden with the perfect arrangement in the territory. His business was lucrative, with his front ranking of vegetable growers in New Mexico. John Mann later purchased thirteen acres of land. With the archbishop's permission, the Jesuits sold the third cemetery property named Campo Santo north of San Felipe de Neri Church on Carnuel Road (Mountain Road) north of the Albuquerque Museum and Tiquex Park, which was no longer used. No graves had been tended or marked from 1854 to 1869, but John made the agreement that he would transport any bones found. He built a home and began his own truck farm on the property north of Blueher Gardens. Herman's piece of ground was cultivated exclusively for vegetables, including twenty-five thousand square feet in hot beds. The water for the farm was in the center of property and was popular for swimming, boating and fishing. They employed an irrigation system drawing water from the Rio Grande using force pumps, steam engines and windmills. Blueher had a capacity of 100,000 pounds of vegetables. He also maintained an onion storage plant with thick walls holding a layer of ashes for a non-conductor of heat. The temperature had to be frigid and the space kept with five employees who were constantly busy with sorting and packing vegetables for delivery in the territory and eight states. Blueher attainted an excellent reputation as an onion raiser. He employed twenty men continually with a monthly payroll of $600. After his success of farming and business, he accumulated a fortune.

In 1884, he married Sophia Spinner from Washington County, Missouri, and they had five children. In 1898, he built a two-story Queen Anne red brick mansion on the northeast corner of the plaza on Short Street (San Felipe Street). The mansion was grand for its time with a high hipped roof with gable dormers, porches on both levels, heated water, acetylene gas electricity, etched glass doors and interior pine woodwork stained to look like oak. It was also the first to have a walk-in closet and a magnificent staircase.

Blueher House. *Personal collection by Debra Montoya, 2022.*

Servants reached the second story using their own staircase in the rear of the home. It was the prettiest and most modern residence for the time. It is recorded as a historic landmark described as "Italianate" by the Historic Landmarks Survey of Albuquerque. It was also listed in the State Register of Cultural Properties as part of Old Albuquerque Historic District in 1979.

In 1891, Blueher was one of the founders of St. Paul's Lutheran Church. In 1897, he became an advocate of the tobacco industry for New Mexico. He proposed with his knowledge that the soil and climate could raise a fine grade of tobacco. His knowledge proved the pursuit of agriculture in New Mexico to the greatest excellence and success. Herman Blueher was known as the first to own a truck in Old Albuquerque. On September 4, 1928, Herman Blueher died in Albuquerque. Sophia Blueher, his widow, later remarried as Mrs. George Stephenson.

Today, the mansion is visible from the plaza but hardly noticeable. It was modified during the Puebloization of Old Town in the 1950s as Queen Anne with Pueblo Revival. The Victorian roof with Queen Anne shingles was removed so the house would blend with neighboring buildings. The porches were removed, the brickwork was covered with stucco to imitate

Blueher House (former La Hacienda), front street view. *Personal collection by Debra Montoya, 2022.*

adobe and a portico with rough exposed posts, beams, vigas and latillas was added to the front facing the plaza. Though the building was stripped of its original beauty and details, the remains are still visible behind the home. The Blueher Mansion was adapted for use as a restaurant in 1952 by the Brown family, previous owners of the first La Placita Dining Rooms inside the original Ambrosio Armijo house. It was known as La Hacienda until 2020, when the business closed permanently. As of September 2022, it is operating as a new business, Ezra's Taste of Home.

Chapter 8

AMBROSIO ARMIJO HOUSE

200 San Felipe Street (Short Street)

Ambrosio Armijo was born in Los Poblanos, Albuquerque, New Mexico, in 1817. He was the son of Juan Nepomuceno Armijo and Maria Rosalia Ortega, from a prominent family. They were married on May 7, 1809, at San Felipe de Neri Catholic Church and had three living sons, Juan Cristobal, Ambrosio and Cristobal Armijo. Ambrosio was also the nephew of General Manuel Armijo, the last provincial Mexican governor of New Mexico under the Mexican Republic (1837–46). Ambrosio married Maria Candelaria Otero Chaves, daughter of Vicente Antonio de la Encarnacion Otero and Maria Gertrudis Duran, in Tome, Valencia, New Mexico, in 1844. Maria was the sister of Antonio J. Otero, one of three Superior Court justices appointed by General Stephen V. Kearny at the beginning of his military government of the New Mexico Territory on September 22, 1846. Ambrosio and Maria had nine children, but unfortunately, Maria passed away in 1858.

A year later, he remarried Maria Candelaria Griego de Romero, daughter of Jose Gabriel Griego and Maria Eulogia Romero, born on February 7, 1834, in Santa Fe. They were married on December 7, 1859, and had twelve children. Ambrosio was born to a wealthy farming community in Los Poblanos Ranch, north of Old Albuquerque. He and his brothers inherited a substantial part of the Elena Gallegos land grant through the nineteenth century, owning five hundred acres of ranch land in Los Poblanos, north of Old Alburquerque. He was the wealthiest businessperson in Old Alburquerque. He owned a ranch in Los Poblanos, Casa Armijo (La

Armijo House
and Store, 1938.
*Albuquerque Museum,
gift of William and
Christine Astholz
PA2002.009.015.*

Placita), Old Alburquerque, a home in Santa Fe, numerous property lots and additions, a mercantile store and later Hotel Armijo. He was also a rancher, owning thousands of sheep and often traveling to other states.

He was also a politician and public servant, contributing to the expansion and repair of San Felipe de Neri Church, as well as commissioner for raising funds for training and education for the youth. He served as vice president for the Pacific Railroad movement, which incorporated the addition of the railroad advantages of a central route in the territory for travel and transportation. He fought with the Union side in the Civil War, obtaining the rank of colonel in the New Mexico Territorial Militia. He served as Bernalillo County probate judge (1863–65) and Bernalillo County treasurer in 1864. In 1852, Ambrosio traveled to California with sheep and returned with $10,000 in six-sided gold coins sewn into his vest. That same year, he traveled to California, and according to the *Santa Fe Weekly Gazette* of September 24, 1853, "Ambrosio Armijo, who took sheep to California last year, lost as many as eleven hundred, among the sand-hills west of the Colorado, by sinking in the sand, and being run over by those behind."

He was a well-known trader on the Santa Fe and Chihuahua Trails, often traveling to Mexico on his trading ventures. In 1864, nomadic Native Americans robbed his wagon on the Santa Fe Trail. In 1876, he traveled to Philadelphia to attend the Centennial Exposition as a merchant known for his merchandising in Old Albuquerque. Ambrosio purchased Casa Armijo in 1844 from his cousin El Colorado Don Juan Armijo Y Maestas. The home was built in 1706 by the Armijo family, four years before the founding of the Villa of Albuquerque, and was the first home in Old Albuquerque. The home is a classic placita (little square) style built for defense in case of attack by raiding nomadic Native Americans. It has massive two-foot-thick adobe walls and one entrance. It is an enclosed placita-style building extending north and southeast, with home portals

La Placita in Casa de Armijo, circa 1955. *Albuquerque Museum, gift of John Borradaile Colligan PA1989.017.058.*

surrounding the small square located at the rear of the present La Placita restaurant on the southeast corner. It has a covered water well furnishing water supply in the center of the placita. Ambrosio lent the use of the existing south wing of the home as a school building for a brief time, allowing the Jesuits to teach classes until the opening of Our Lady of the Angels School on September 21, 1881.

Ambrosio built a joint residence and business addition on the east side corner of the plaza on Short Street (200 San Felipe Street) in 1880, connecting to the original property of Casa Armijo. The front of the house with store is one hundred feet long in classic placita style. It originally consisted of two square-shaped buildings with a pitched and gabled roof, joined by a passageway in the center with the original Casa Armijo. The adobe structure has door and window frames of milled lumber and a gabled roof. The front had an Italianate portico of semicircular arches supported with slender wooden columns. The home interior had whitewashed walls redone every year by the servants and with constant re-plastering. There were also large vigas all along the front of the house and store. The elaborate carved furniture was upholstered with horsehair. A large square Steinway piano was covered with an adorned Mexican blanket (Saltillo). The Armijo women wore beautiful, elaborate dresses with fine jewelry provided by Ambrosio Armijo.

The second story was added in 1882 to please his daughter Maria Teresa with a room on the second level, above the staircase. The magnificent walnut staircase was added for her wedding day to marry Dr. John Symington of Maryland. It was built to showcase her beautiful wedding gown with a long train down the staircase and walking across the plaza to San Felipe Church to the marriage ceremony. Prior to the marriage, Maria Teresa, twenty-one, returned to her father's home from St. Louis, Missouri, trained in the arts by nuns from the Visitation Convent. She was known as unattractive, joyful, popular and happy. She was a graceful dancer, an expert horse rider and a pianist. Soon, her male admirers came visiting from Las Vegas, Las Cruces and Santa Fe. Only one admirer caught her eye: Dr. John Symington, tall, blond and charming. He arrived in Old Albuquerque on the Santa Fe Trail with Mr. Staab, Sister Augustine and Sister Blandina as a teamster to protect the sisters in June 1877. At the time, Billy the Kid was attacking and robbing coaches on the trail. Dr. Symington and Maria Teresa met while riding. Her father, Ambrosio, did not consider Symington suitable for his daughter and only knew the young man had come west on the wagon train. Dr. John Symington was later appointed surgeon to the military post in Old Albuquerque. There was also another young male suitor whom Maria Teresa had forgotten, a young Mexican man by the name of Alderete. Maria met him at a friend's house in St. Louis. While her flirtation was harmless, he arrived with his family to marry her. He brought gifts, a fine carriage with her monogram on the door, shawls, laces and jewels. Ambrosio, strict with the conventions of Mexico, said she would have to marry the young man, for she had misled him and honor demanded she fulfill his expectations. Wedding plans proceeded to move forward but had a setback when Alderete attended a huge dance that took place in Alameda neighborhood, resulting in behavior displeasing to Ambrosio, who forbid the marriage to take place. He at once sent Maria Teresa to stay with relatives in Bernalillo, New Mexico, and invited Alderete to visit for a formal close. Dr. John Symington was still present and wanted to marry Maria Teresa, but her father did not favor him. Father Gasparri, from San Felipe de Neri Church, had a talk with Ambrosio, reminding him that Maria Teresa, at twenty-one, could do as she pleased. Soon after, the marriage took place on November 13, 1871, in the elaborate parlor of the Armijo home. Her wedding dress was white satin with a tight bodice and fringe trim. They lived happily, later moving to Baltimore, Maryland.

Ambrosio moved his business interests to New Town (Albuquerque) in June 1880, buying five property lots on Central Avenue (Railroad Avenue) where the Armijo House Hotel was erected. It was the first luxury and leading hotel in New Town, owned by his son Mariano Armijo, and set a high standard for elegance in the territory. It was located at the southwest corner of Railroad (Central) Avenue and Third Street. Built in 1880, it was a spectacular three-story building built as French Second Empire style with a mansard roof and central tower. It was constructed of adobe and wood and cost $25,000 to build. The hotel was opened in the spring of 1881 by Scott Moore, manager, who gave a champagne dinner to guests from Albuquerque, Santa Fe, Las Vegas, Denver and other cities. He was committed to making it the best in the territory and succeeded. Male patrons were required to wear coats in the dining room; if they did not have one, the hotel supplied an alpaca jacket for the evening. Wyatt Earp, Doc Holliday and Pat Garrett were guests. After the opening of the hotel, Ambrosio bought the property and built the addition known as the Ambrosio Armijo Hall. The Armijo House Hotel was destroyed by fire on February 10, 1897.

Unfortunately, Ambrosio passed away on April 10, 1882, leaving the care of his children and estate to his wife, Maria Armijo, at age forty-nine. Maria remarried Charles Bernhardt Ruppe, a twenty-year-old German immigrant from Manhattan, New York City. The engagement and marriage were a scandal, and the Armijo children (Jesus, Mariano, Sheriff Perfecto and Elias) claimed that the estate was an incentive for Ruppe. According to the Santa Fe New Mexican of August 11, 1883:

The pending engagement of marriage announced by Bernhardt Ruppe, in yesterday morning's Journal *between himself and Mrs. Ambrosio Armijo, has terminated rather suddenly by the departure of Ruppe for parts unknown. The unfortunate occurrence is to be much regretted, especially as it brings into enviable notice one of the most respectable families, of Bernalillo County. With a view of putting a stop to all sensational talk over the matter, the* Journal *man got an account of the material facts in the case for publication.*

The first known of Ruppe by Armijo family was when he was running as news agent between Santa Fe and San Miguel, perhaps nearly two years ago. At the time he formed the acquaintance of Mrs. Jesus Armijo, who next saw him washing dishes in a Railroad Avenue restaurant. He was next employed in a drug store kept by Mr. Kent. Being a smart young man and a bright, ready talker, Jesus Armijo took a liking to him, and got him a position in his father's house as collector. When Don Ambrosio Armijo died, the whole care of children and estate fell to his widow, who during his lifetime never knew what it was to transact any business, or even superintend the affairs of her household. Mrs. Armijo, now advanced to the age of 50 years, weighed down with heavy care, was glad to have assistance tendered her. Mr. Ruppe, a young man possibly not more than 24 or 25 years of age, took advantage of his confidential relations to the family to press a marriage suit to a lady who had a grown son nearly as old as himself. No doubt, Mrs. Armijo's estate was a powerful incentive to the young man. He carried the matter as far, and without the knowledge of the family, as to have the following cards to be printed on Thursday last: "You are respectfully invited to attend the marriage ceremony of Mrs. Candelaria Griega de Armijo to Bernhardt Ruppe, at the San Felipe cathedral, on Tuesday evening, October 30, 1883, at 7 o'clock p.m."

Jesus and Mariano Armijo, who with Sheriff Armijo are stepsons of Mrs. Armijo, and Elias Armijo, her natural son, heard of Ruppe's secret doings Thursday night and were highly incensed over the situation. They soon made up their minds that they would put a stop to his proceeding further in the matter. It was a late hour Thursday night when they reached Ruppe's drug store in old town. Elias Armijo was boiling with rage and fearing that he would shoot Ruppe he was held back by his brothers.

Mariano Armijo called Ruppe quietly to one side and gave him to understand that he should give up the idea he entertained, that he abused the confidence placed in him and had taken undue advantage of the position which he was allowed to occupy towards the family. The brothers also visited Mrs. Armijo, she was easily persuaded of the folly of the proposed marriage and told her sons that such a thing could never occur. One of the brothers said he entertained serious doubts as to her sanity for ever harboring such a proposition. He regarded Ruppe as a mere adventurer.

Mr. Ruppe has but little to say. He denies many of the above stated facts, to be sure: states that his intention was honorable: says it was his intention at first to marry the lady, but after encountering such determined opposition he abandoned all idea of it and has not left Albuquerque for all time. He sent by this afternoon's mail to Albuquerque a power of attorney to Dr. Muehl who will take charge of his drug store and settle all his affairs. Mr. Ruppe may remain in Santa Fe."

Shortly after, records show that a marriage took place on October 9, 1883, at San Felipe de Neri Church. According to the *Las Vegas Daily Gazette* of October 25, 1883:

Bernard Ruppe, who married the widow of Don Ambrosio Armijo, of Albuquerque, was again forced to leave that place. He took refuge at the residence of Don Cristobal Armijo with his wife, and last Sunday night his new wife's son, Elias, and his brother Jesus, went to Don Cristobal's residence broke in the doors and windows and forced Ruppe and Don Cristobal to flee for their lives. They got away and are now at Bernalillo.— Santa Fe Review. *Records indicate the marriage was later annulled.*

Charles B. Ruppe was the founder the B. Ruppe Drug Store at 807 Fourth Street SW, Albuquerque. He later remarried Caroline Fiora Ruppe. Maria Armijo moved to New Town (Albuquerque), and the former Armijo residence was rented for a brief time in 1896 to Jacob Stueckel, a German immigrant and employee of Herman Blueher. Jacob later built a home in 1897 on Short Street (306 San Felipe). In 1906, the Armijo house was sold to Juan Zamora, and for a brief time, it became a dance hall. Zamora later changed his ownership to joint ownership with Beatriz Ruiz, and it became a saloon, gambling house and brothel during the 1920s and 1930s. In 1930, Zamora accepted an offer of $1,000 from Brice and Nelda Sewell, who moved to Old Albuquerque from St. Louis. The Sewells are known for creating and preserving the history of Old Albuquerque. They immediately renovated the property and tore down the second story of the newer house. They restored the original Casa Armijo, which was deteriorating, and made it into a series of apartments. Brice and Nelda Sewell lived in the original part of Casa Armijo for years. In 1935, the north side of the structure was operated as La Placita Dining Rooms by Russell Weirs, with a trading post store. In the early 1940s, Cyrus Brown, an auditor from Chicago, took over the restaurant. He and his wife developed it to the flourishing business of La Placita Dining, with the Elliott family managing since 1951. In 1955, the apartments were converted into a series of little shops with items sold to preserve the quality of Spanish culture. The original part of the Casa Armijo where Brice and Nelda lived was later converted to a shop known for years as shop 1, the Crazy Horse Gallery, operated by Nelda. Nelda was also involved in efforts to allow Native Americans from all pueblo reservations to sell their crafts undisturbed in the front of La Placita building, keeping their historic rights and customs since the founding of the city of Albuquerque in 1706. The remaining shops are known today as Patio Market, operating with ten retail shops: Yucca Art Gallery, Dancing Crow, Ghost Wolf Gallery, Allen Aragon Gallery, Nikki Zabicki's, Amy Janes Cool Stuff, Black Bird

Coffee House, Photographs by Butch Phillips, Desert Bird Mercantile and Guerrilla Graphix. It is managed and leased by Berger Briggs.

It is registered as a historic landmark, described as Territorial style by the Historic Survey of Albuquerque. It was also listed in the State Register of Cultural Properties as part of the Old Albuquerque Historic District in 1979. A bronze plaque furnished by the Albuquerque Historical Society was dedicated to La Placita for the site of the Armijo Hacienda, which dates to the founding of Albuquerque in 1706. It was most known as the home of Ambrosio Armijo for many years but dates to the early members of the Armijo family. The Armijo family are significant to the history of Old Albuquerque (Old Town Plaza) as original early settlers and wealthy, prominent, respectable families in the territory. Ambrosio Armijo was honorable in his efforts to serve numerous political roles, as well as involved in business, community and San Felipe de Neri Church. He was also one of the richest men in New Mexico Territory. On April 26, 2004, for the Tri-Centennial Celebration, Mayor Martin Chavez had a memorial plaque installed on a lamppost in Old Town Plaza honoring Ambrosio Armijo as a merchant and landowner for his contributions to both Old and New Town Albuquerque.

Today, the residence is visible from the plaza. It escaped the Puebloization of the 1950s as Territorial and Pueblo Revival style. The Sanborn Insurance maps of 1891 through 1931 show the building to have had numerous renovations, additions, razings and reconstruction. A major building alteration in the 1930 resulted in the removal of the gabled roof to the north.

La Placita. *Personal collection by Debra Montoya, 2022.*

The exterior is now stucco. The Italianate portico was replaced as Spanish Colonial style with rough-hewn posts, beams and corbel brackets. Several stores on the south and west sides have ceiling features that are original with rough-hewn beams. The flooring was replaced with red brick, including the outside pathways. On the south side, one store has an early Spanish Colonial kiva-style fireplace, which was a later addition. The water well has been re-stuccoed and still operates, with many locals and tourists throwing in coins for well wishes. The massive gate at the west entrance to the placita was removed after 1941. The construction is an excellent example of the Spanish colonial placita plan designed to be defensible in case of an attack. Unfortunately, La Placita restaurant closed in 2020 and is currently vacant.

Chapter 9

CHARLES BOTTGER HOUSE

110 San Felipe NW (Short Street)

Charles August Bottger was born on August 27, 1872, in New York City. He was the son of Louis Friedrich Bottger and Julia Louisa Muehling, immigrants from Germany and residents of New York City who married on September 19, 1871. Charles moved from Rutherford, New Jersey, to Old Albuquerque in 1889 to invest in the Rio Puerco land company. He liked New Mexico and decided to stay and found work at the Post Hotel, owned by Thomas Post. Charles's occupation was a capitalist, and he was known for his innovative methods with first-class features. He was brilliant in his business affairs and public interests. He was born into a wealthy family, and when he decided to stay in Old Albuquerque, he also owned real estate in Rutherford, New Jersey.

Thomas Post, a stagecoach driver born in Essex, New Jersey, came down the Santa Fe Trail from Kansas in the 1860s. He married Maria Gertrudis Garcia, from the Atrisco neighborhood south of Old Albuquerque, on December 30, 1872. She was a widow of Jose Baca with a daughter, Maria Miquela Baca, born in 1859. As New Albuquerque was growing, crossing the Rio Grande became necessary to folks. Thomas began a ferry service in 1874, and on December 12, 1882, he constructed a pontoon bridge on the site of the present-day bridge on Central Avenue NW. The tollhouse, grocery store and home were located on the center of the bridge. The fee to cross the bridge was five cents per person on foot, with no trotting allowed. The Rio Grande was treacherous, as the sand constantly moved

Bottger house in the snow, circa 1935. *Albuquerque Museum, gift of Charmaigne Gallegos Riehl PA2000.052.001.*

and required much labor. On May 29, 1885, spring floodwaters washed away the bridge, including the Posts' home and grocery store, destroying all their possessions. The Albuquerque Bridge Company, incorporated in 1879, built another toll bridge across the Rio Grande with a tollhouse placed in the middle of the structure.

After the toll bridge washed away their home and belongings, Thomas Post purchased the Exchange Hotel. The site occupied one of the oldest buildings in Old Albuquerque, a one-story adobe structure south of the plaza on Short Street (San Felipe Street) and Railroad Avenue (Central Avenue). The Armijo family had previously operated a general store in the building prior to the Mexican-American War (1846–48), and it was later converted into an inn known as the Exchange Hotel. Thomas reopened the hotel and changed the name to Post Exchange Hotel, which proved to turn its fortune around. It became a favored stop in Old Albuquerque. His rates were $1.50 per day for transient boarders and $7.00 per week for board and room for regular boarders. After the death of Thomas Post on July 12, 1893, Maria Miquela Post, his stepdaughter, acquired the property. Miquela remarried a third time to Charles A. Bottger in September 1897, and they had two daughters, Julia and Dorothy Bottger. Charles Bottger took over the operation of his father-in-law's hotel property and converted it into the Sunnyside Inn, which included a new form of amusement to the locals: the first bowling alley. It also had a private club with first-class music, outdoor patio dining, a concert garden with a seating capacity of 450 people with half accommodated with tables and a bandstand on the rooftop for a better quality of sound. Admission was free, but customers were expected to drink. In later years, the former Sunnyside Inn became the San Felipe Club, offering drinks and women during the Prohibition years with a row of small apartments in the rear of the building. In later years, it became an art gallery, museum and trash collection company, but it was damaged by fire and razed in 1960.

Years later, Charles and Miquela bought property east of the Sunnyside Inn at the corner of Railroad Avenue (Central Avenue) and Short Street (San Felipe Street) from Cristobal Armijo before his death. It was the former property site of Mexican governor Don Manuel Armijo's forty-room hacienda, which was sold to Don Cristobal Armijo and leased to the United States for officers' quarters. It was also known as the family

Rio Grande Bridge, circa 1890. *Albuquerque Museum, gift of Center for Southwest Research, University of New Mexico PA1978.050.533.*

Manuel Armijo residence, circa 1905. *Albuquerque Museum, gift of Historic Albuquerque Inc. PA2019.023.002.*

residence of Irene Rucker Sheridan, wife of Philip Henry Sheridan, lieutenant general of the United States Army in 1884. Irene Rucker was born in 1856 in Fort Union, New Mexico (Indian Territory known as Oklahoma), and was the daughter of Brigadier General Daniel H. Rucker, who was the quartermaster general of the army with the rank of brigadier general and assigned to the Albuquerque Garrison as the quartermaster. He was also one of the officers who escorted President Lincoln's body from the Peterson House to the White House following his death in April 1865.

While Philip Henry Sheridan was stationed in Old Albuquerque, he would often inspect the residence where he believed his wife, Irene Rucker Sheridan, was born. Although her two younger sisters were born in the former hacienda, she was not. Philip and Irene were married on June 3, 1875—he was forty-four and she was nineteen—and they had four children, including twin daughters. Philip and his wife relocated to Washington, D.C., and lived in a large home on Rhode Island Avenue and Seventieth Street given to them by Chicago citizens in appreciation of General Sheridan's protection of the city after the Great Chicago Fire in

1871. Philip died on August 5, 1888, due to heart failure and was buried at Arlington National Cemetery. Irene Sheridan never remarried and spent time between both homes as well as at her family summer cottage in Nonquitt, Massachusetts. On February 24, 1938, Irene Rucker Sheridan died and was buried with her husband at Arlington National Cemetery. Philip Sheridan is the only person featured on a ten-dollar U.S Treasury note issued in 1890 and 1891. An image of his chest reappeared on the five-dollar silver certificate in 1896.

In 1910, Charles demolished the old forty-room hacienda and started construction on a new home at Short Street (110 San Felipe Street). He built a two-and-a-half-story concrete mansion with a basement designed by Edward B. Christy, who was also responsible for the remodeling of the University of New Mexico's Hodgin Hall in 1908. The home was the first to have a red tile Mediterranean-style roof; it also had a large open floor space for its time, a large wraparound porch, a basement, mahogany woodwork and glazing, gas lighting, speaking tubes to all rooms, pressed-tin ceilings in three main rooms, a dumbwaiter to the upper floor, a fireplace and a coal-fired central heater. The Bottger mansion was known as the Pride of Old Town after it was built. Charles lived in the mansion for four years until his death on December 19, 1914. After his death, Miquela started taking in boarders as income. She continued living in the mansion for many years until her death on February 29, 1936, in Santa Fe. Her living daughter, Julia Bottger Gallegos, married to George Gallegos, inherited the mansion with their children. In the 1940s, Julia converted the first floor to a Mexican restaurant named El Encato, where she personally prepared and served food. George Gallegos Jr. painted the walls with beautiful murals. A large self-playing Ozen piano was brought from Kansas City to the mansion, where Julia would often play. Julia held tea in the mansion, honoring Senator Dennis Chavez and other political candidates, including her husband, George Gallegos, who ran successfully for precinct judge. He served as justice of the peace in Old Town and had many visitors.

In the 1940s, the FBI's most wanted criminal, Machine Gun Kelly, was being pursued by officers when he decided to check in at the Bottger mansion with his girlfriend and gang under assumed names. After several days, the owners became suspicious when a neighborhood boy was sent out daily to buy meals and deliver them back to their rooms. The police were notified, and the outlaws quickly left the mansion but were captured shortly after and imprisoned. In 1956, Elvis Presley, Bill Black and Scotty Moore performed two shows in Albuquerque and stayed at the Bottger mansion.

Bottger Mansion bed-and-breakfast. *Personal collection by Debra Montoya, 2022.*

In the late 1950s, Frank Sinatra was a guest attending a prominent Italian family wedding and performed in the courtyard.

Today, the Bottger Mansion is visible from Old Town Plaza as Mediterranean and Italianate style. Unlike all the other homes in Old Albuquerque, this home was not modified during the Puebloization of Old Town in the 1950s as Italianate style because of its distance to the plaza. It maintained the simple square floor plan, but original textures have been covered with pink stucco with a few lost original details. A glassed sunporch now wraps around the south and east sides of the home, with a smaller projecting sunporch on the north side. The Charles A. Bottger House was listed in the New Mexico State Register of Cultural Properties on October 26, 1979. It was listed in the U.S. National Register of Historic Places on March 7, 1983, and is the only lodging accommodation in Old Town Historic District. It is also registered as a historic landmark, described as "Italianate" by the Historic Landmarks Survey of Albuquerque. On April 26, 2004, for the Tri-Centennial Celebration, Mayor Martin Chavez had a memorial plaque installed on a lamppost in Old Town Plaza honoring Charles Bottger and Thomas Post for contributing to both Old and New Town Albuquerque.

Julia Bottger, a daughter, in 1966 graciously donated a piece of the Bottger land, where the present San Felipe School grounds are today. Julia Bottger Gallegos died on May 21, 1968. In 1970, a family dispute relating to the inheritance of the property left the mansion vacant for years, and it was sold outside the family. Years later, it operated as an art gallery, restaurant and beauty parlor. Today, it is known as Bottger Mansion, operating as a bed-and-breakfast since 1989.

Chapter 10

CRISTOBAL ARMIJO HOUSE

2004 South Plaza NW (James Street)

Juan Cristobal Armijo was born in 1810 in Ranchos de Albuquerque, Bernalillo County. He was the son of Juan Nepomuceno Armijo and Rosalia Ortega, from a prominent family. They were married on May 7, 1809, at San Felipe de Neri Catholic Church and had three living sons, Juan Cristobal, Ambrosio and Cristobal Armijo. Juan Cristobal was the nephew of General Manuel Armijo, the Mexican governor of New Mexico, who was in command of the territory when the United States acquired the country. The former residence of General Manuel Armijo was a forty-room hacienda located at the corner of Railroad Avenue (Central Avenue) and Short Street (San Felipe Street). It was later sold to Cristobal Armijo and leased to the United States for officers' quarters. It is known as the residence of Philip Henry Sheridan, lieutenant general of United States Army in 1884.

On April 17, 1830, Juan Cristobal married Juana Maria Chavez, daughter of Governor Francisco Xavier II Duran Y Chaves, the wealthiest Spaniard in the country, and they had nineteen children. Juan Cristobal was born to a wealthy farming community in Los Poblanos Ranch north of Old Albuquerque and was a member of Albuquerque's influential Armijo family. He had a distinguished career of public service and private enterprise. During the 1850s, he resided with his family in north Albuquerque, where he also had a mercantile store. Bringing goods into Mexico direct from the States, he maintained his business for many years and succeeded in building a large fortune. Juan Cristobal and his brothers inherited a substantial portion of

South Plaza Street, circa 1915. Cristobal Armijo House is at far left. *Albuquerque Museum, gift of John Airy PA1982.180.845.*

the Elena Gallegos land grant through the nineteenth century, owning five hundred acres of ranch land in Los Poblanos north of Old Albuquerque. In the early 1840s, he traveled to St. Louis to enter the freighting business between Albuquerque and Chihuahua, Mexico. He was also an investor and founder of the First National Bank in 1881 in New Town (Albuquerque), serving as director.

Cristobal fought by the side of Governor Perez as a brave and courageous soldier. This marked the close of Mexican ruling in the territory. Years later, he received a commission as colonel in the Mexican army preceding the Mexican War (1846–48), which led to his command against the Navajo Native Americans in 1840. He invaded their territory and was successful in capturing prisoners, horses and head of sheep that had been stolen by the Navajo. When the Mexican army was defeated in the war of 1844–46, he became a patriotic American citizen, joined the New Mexico militia and United States Army in 1846 and advanced to the rank of Colonel. He represented Bernalillo County as a member of the First Territorial Legislature of New Mexico Territory in 1851, serving in the House, and was reelected to the same body in 1852, serving the second assembly. He was again reelected to the seventh assembly. During the Civil War, he held a commission with the New Mexico militia and participated in the Battle of Val Verde, defending Fort Craig. In later years, he made several expeditions against the Native Americans, where he met with success.

Juan Cristobal and the Juana early family residence was known as Hacienda del Lago. It was located in Los Griegos neighborhood north of Old Albuquerque at 207 Griegos Road NW and was built between 1875 and 1885. It was a hacienda with an enclosed patio and a zaguan entrance that leads into a placita and four square single-file rooms. The estate was valued at $110,000 in 1860. The property was listed in the New Mexico State Register of Cultural Properties on January 20, 1978, and the U.S. National Register of Historic Places on September 30, 1982. It is also registered as a historic landmark described as Territorial style from the Historic Landmarks Survey of Albuquerque. Juan Cristobal started construction to build a new home in Old Albuquerque in Italianate and Queen Anne styles on the southeast corner of the plaza on James Street (2004 South Plaza NW) in 1883. He built a two-story square adobe home with a truncated roof with projecting cornice with paired brackets, an extended balustrade on the upper-story balcony, a wrapped porch around the north and east sides with supported Queen Anne–style posts and fan-shaped bracing. The lower story was plastered and carved with paint to have the appearance of brick. The second story had actual brick facing applied to the front. The rear of the home had an adobe corral with a zaguan entrance. It is recorded as a historic landmark described as "Territorial Adobe, Brick Face." It is also in the State Register of Cultural Properties as part of Old Albuquerque Historic District in 1979.

According to folklore, before there was a bank in the territory, Juan Cristobal hid his money in the adobe walls and plastered over them. He would dig it out once a year to send to a bank in Chihuahua, Mexico. Documentation states he forgot some places where he hid the money, and people have searched for it without success. However, a few artifacts were discovered inside the walls. Furthermore, there is an existing secret tunnel under the house that years ago may have led to the home of his brother Ambrosio Armijo (La Placita restaurant). According to the book *Ghosts of Old Town Albuquerque* by Cody Polston:

> *The area below was a large crawlspace, about three feet in width and four feet high, and could be more accurately described as a tunnel. The tunnel itself had several inches of lime on the floor and extended northward toward the front of the building for about fifteen feet. At this point, it turned and headed east. As I traveled down the east section, the floor began to rise until the crawlspace was impassable. In this location, I found huge deposits of bones covering the floor, at least one foot in depth.*

Upon further investigation from Polston, "samples of the bones were taken for professional analysis. The bones were determined to be goat bones, about two hundred years old."

Juan Cristobal Armijo died on December 27, 1884, at the age of seventy-four. He left his property—including Hacienda del Lago (old homestead), his Old Albuquerque home on James Street (2004 South Plaza), a vineyard and La Milpa (cornfield)—to his widow, Juana. After her death in 1888, the property was divided among the children and other relatives. The Armijo family is significant to the history of Old Albuquerque (Old Town Plaza) as original early settlers, prominent and respectable families in the territory. Juan Cristobal was one of the most successful businesspeople and investors in the territory and had a reputation of integrity and honor.

Today, the Cristobal Armijo house is visible from the plaza but barely noticeable. It was modified during the Puebloization of Old Town in the 1950s as Italianate, Queen Anne and Pueblo Revival. The exterior has been covered with stucco; the segmental arched windows are hidden; the cornice detail brick has been covered; the hipped roof has been flattened; and the original wraparound porch on the east and north sides, with upper-story balustrade supported with Queen Anne posts and fan-shaped bracing, has been removed. The newly Spanish Colonial additions are rough-hewn posts, beams, corbel brackets and projecting vigas. The interior has been remodeled over the years, with wood floors and wood beam ceilings.

In the 1930s, the property was purchased by Florencio Zamora as a private residence and known to locals as La Mansion Historical de Zamora,

Cristobal Armijo house. *Personal collection by Debra Montoya, 2022.*

with generations of children and grandchildren born in the home. Zamora maintained a butcher shop before his death in 1946. He left the residence to his grandson Florencio Chavez, and it served as a residence and housed the Perfume of the Desert shop and Indian Curio Store. Through the years, it has housed La Plaza Primorosa Gift Shop, Old Town Trading Post and the Casa de Fiesta restaurant, and today, it operates as Mercado Plaza, selling gifts, rugs, clothing and souvenirs. The current owner is Tito Chavez, great-grandson of Florencio Zamora, former owner of the Florencio Grocery Store and Butcher Shop at 301 Romero Street NW. Tito Chavez is the only surviving family member of the early settlers to own a property in Old Town Plaza.

Chapter 11

MANUEL SPRINGER HOUSE

2036 South Plaza (James Street)

Manuel R. Springer was born on November 29, 1871, in Old Albuquerque. He was the son of Henry Springer, from Wurttemberg, Germany, and Placida Saavedra, who were married on March 20, 1875. Manuel married Carlotta Garcia on May 16, 1892. Carlotta was the daughter of Manuel Garcia, sheriff of Bernalillo County, and Maria Andrea de Jesus Perea. Manuel and Carlotta had six children.

Manuel R. Springer started in business at an early age after the death of his father, Henry. Manuel established a mercantile store as a grocery and merchandiser in 1895 at the same business location as his father. He attained a large supply as a merchant to serve the territory and remained successful for the duration of his business and personal life. Manuel was appointed county commissioner in November 1904. He built a residence on James Street (2036 South Plaza) on the plaza in 1909. The home construction adjoined his father's mercantile store. Manuel built a Queen Anne two-story red brick home with a hipped roof and dormer vents. It featured a projecting tower of bay windows on the southwest and northwest sides of the second level.

At midnight on the night of May 14, 1913, Manuel and his wife had an encounter at their doorstep with a mysterious woman who spoke perfect English, said she was an Egyptian and was attired in a gypsy costume. According to the *Albuquerque Evening Herald* of May 15, 1913:

Demecio Delgadillo is innocent of murder
Manuel R. Springer, a member of the Board of County Commissioners
of Bernalillo County, and a Prominent Merchant of Old Albuquerque,
was so deeply impressed by the appearance of the unknown visitor that he
assisted in the circulation of a petition appealing to Governor McDonald to
commute the death penalty to life imprisonment. Mr. Springer was strangely
affected and unnerved by the mysterious appearance of the woman at his
residence in Old Town last night and frankly admitted today that he was
terribly frightened. "I warn you not to hang this man" was the warning of
the woman who said she was an Egyptian. "I tell you he is not guilty. I
know the parties that killed the woman." The woman disappeared suddenly
from the porch of the Springer home and efforts by Mr. Springer to trace
her today proved unsuccessful. "It was just about midnight where I was
awakened by my wife, said Mr. Springer today. The electric bell upstairs
was ringing and ringing. I flashed on the lights upstairs and in the hall
below. I descended the stairs and switched on the porch lights. Going to the
front door I peered outside through the curtain, there stood a woman, whom
I never saw before. She was dressed like a gypsy.

"The woman was agitated and apparently excited. I called out, asking
her what she wished. She answered back: 'I am an Egyptian, I came to tell
you and warn you not to hang this man, I tell you he is not guilty. I know
the parties that killed the woman.' I shouted back to her that I had nothing
to do with the hanging of the man. She then repeated her warning a second
time, using the same word as before. I stood shivering in the reception room,
still looking out at the woman. It was a bright moonlight and I switched off
the porch light. The woman remained there, I was much frightened and did
not know what to do. Then for the third time, she uttered the warning, in the
same manner as before. Her face twitched and she trembled as she spoke. I
stood in the reception a moment longer, hesitating what to do. I didn't know
the woman and have absolutely nothing to do with the care of prisoners.
While I was debating whether to take a chance and go outside and attempt
to find out the identity of the woman, she disappeared, walking rapidly
down the porch stairs, into the front yard and out into the street. My theory
is that she mistook my house for the house of Sheriff Jesus Romero, who
lives several doors from me. The appearance of the woman and the warning
she spoke made a deep impression on me. I would be inclined to doubt my
own senses but the fact, that my wife, alarmed at the insistent ringing
of the doorbell, and the commotion that followed. Had come halfway
downstairs and plainly heard what the woman said to me. My wife was

Old Town, with the Manuel Springer property in center left, circa 1880. *Albuquerque Museum, gift of Scytha Motto PA1978.077.003.*

much frightened and was at a loss to explain the occurrence and unable to identify the woman. We are much worried by the affair and would be glad if we could clear up the mystery and discover what significance attaches to it. I am almost positive that the woman was not a Mexican and she did not have a Spanish accent."

Manuel Springer died on November 11, 1917. His funeral service took place on November 14 at San Felipe de Neri Church, and according to the *Albuquerque Morning Journal* of November 15, 1917:

The funeral of Manuel Springer, held from the San Felipe de Neri church in Old Albuquerque yesterday morning, was one of the largest ever held in either the old or new city. The procession following the services was estimated to be more than a mile long. Many persons unable to gain entrance to the church stood outside throughout the services. High mass of requiem was held, Father Di Pietro officiating. The offices in the county courthouse were closed in the morning. The floral offerings were numerous with an extensive line of carriages and automobiles, members of the Old Town fraternal society marched in the procession. Burial was in Santa Barbara cemetery.

His wife, Carlotta, later remarried on September 13, 1919, to Teofilo Padilla and remained living in the residence for many years.

Today, the Manuel Springer home is partially visible from the plaza. It was modified during the Puebloization of Old Town in the 1950s as Queen Anne and Pueblo Revival style. The residence is set back from the street front, which conceals the original home. The later additions to the property include a single-story storefront and a two-story portal, which forms an open walkway to the residence's second level. The walkway conceals the bay window at the northwest corner. The brick now has stucco and is painted white with rough-hewn portico and blue trim. The interior has retained its original structure and flooring. It is registered as a historic landmark, described as "Queen Anne" by the Historic Landmarks Survey of Albuquerque. It was also listed in the State Register of Cultural Properties as part of Old Albuquerque Historic District in 1979.

During the Depression, it served as a rooming house. Mr. and Mrs. James Bennett purchased the property in 1943. James managed the *Old Town Gazette* and served as a church official during the Old Town fiestas. They

Manuel Springer house and covered wagon. *Personal collection by Debra Montoya, 2022.*

remodeled and preserved the upper level as their residence while using the lower level as commercial space operating as La Cocina, serving elegant dining and famous for its Mexican, Italian and charcoal broiled steaks for many years. The restaurant was adjacent with both properties on the lower level and featured paintings on the walls. One was a painting of the plaza dated 1885, by an artist named Trousset. The painting was owned by Erna Fergusson, granddaughter of Franz Huning. Erna was an organizer of the Old Albuquerque Historical Society. Another painting featured the duke of Alburquerque, who was viceroy of New Spain at the time Albuquerque was founded; it was painted by artist Lloyd Goff. The building has been operating as the Covered Wagon since 1959 as one of the largest stores in Old Town Plaza.

Chapter 12

HENRY SPRINGER STORE

2038 South Plaza (James Street)

Henry Springer was born on June 15, 1831, in Wurttemberg, Germany. In 1850, his parents, Myer and Charlotte Springer, immigrated to the United States with sons Henry and Levi to Lafayette, Missouri. After the death of his parents in 1861, Henry moved to Santa Fe, where he operated a hotel for two years. In 1863, he moved to Old Albuquerque, where he opened a mercantile store operating as a grocery store, one of three that existed in the town. Henry was a successful and brilliant businessperson, merchant with local and commercial affairs, landowner and liquor merchant and had many public interests for many years while he made Old Albuquerque his home.

On March 20, 1875, he married Placida Saavedra; she was previously married to John Hunick, who went off to the Civil War. Together, Placida and John had three children. Henry and Placida had eight children during their marriage. Henry constructed a new building for his store in 1880 on the west side of the plaza on James Street (2038 South Plaza). It was one of the earliest brick structures. It was a single-story red brick structure with a clipped corner entrance with large windows and cornice detailed brick on the rooftop edge and a portal entrance. His mercantile store was flourishing, and he was becoming wealthy and successful with his business, commercial affairs and public interests. Henry opened a second mercantile store in Springfield, Arizona, also known as Round Valley. He was supplying blanket production to sell his merchandise to the army at Fort Apache in 1873. The fort needed consumer products for the territory, including grain,

James Street, with the Henry Springer house at lower left and the Mint Saloon, circa 1882. *Albuquerque Museum, gift of Center for Southwest Research, University of New Mexico PA1978.050.038.*

cattle, charcoal, wood and other consumables. Round Valley soon became a magnet for entrepreneurs, including Henry Springer on April 18, 1876. He opened a large mercantile store and contracted grain in Round Valley the same year. Oren W. McCullough donated the land for him to build his store and home.

The *Republican Review* of May 13, 1876, reported, "Henry had established a large mercantile house and several 'substantial houses' that were under construction on May 10, 1876, the town site was officially named 'Springerville,' Arizona." Henry opened a third branch mercantile store on the Rio Puerco at San Ignacio on May 20, 1876. At the same time, Henry hired a manager named Don Antonio Jose Herrera, who reported in the *Republican Review* of May 20, 1876, "His business is increasing at such a rate the old quarters have become too small to accommodate the large amount of goods he is obliged to store." Henry was one of the leading merchants in the territory. At one time, he also owned the Springer addition, comprising seventy-four town lots (between Fourth and Sixth Streets, between Cooper and Tijeras Streets) in New Albuquerque, which he was successful for years.

Henry Springer house.
Personal collection by Debra
Montoya, 2022.

In 1877, he overextended himself, losing $30,000 on barley crops to meet government contracts on capital investments he had previously negotiated. Creditors such as France Huning and Spiegelburg started to call in his debts, and Henry was unable to cover them. There were numerous commentaries about Henry Springer's financial difficulties.

The *Weekly Arizona Miner* of Prescott noted on April 13, 1877, that "Mr. Springer's present embarrassment is caused by having several thousand dollars tied up in barley; which he has been unable to dispose of." His bookkeeper, James Roberts, died under mysterious circumstances, apparently a suicide involving an overdose of chloral hydrate, morphine and wine.

On January 23, 1879, his wife Placida Saavedra Springer, died, leaving behind eleven children. After her death, Henry went to work for his former competitor Franz Huning in his store as a salesman. In May 1879, he had managed to work his way out from under the insolvency court in Santa Fe and recuperated his losses. He was successful in starting a new business venture as owner and operator of the Mint saloon, operating as a liquor merchant on the corner of Main Street (Rio Grande Boulevard) and James Street

(South Plaza). The saloon was popular with a monarch billiard table and cozy clubroom with the best wines, liquors and cigars in the city. According to Old Albuquerque folklore, the house was a speakeasy and brothel during Prohibition. In later years, Henry's home residence was in the neighborhood of Duranes, north of Old Albuquerque, until his death on April 7, 1882, at fifty-one. He left eleven children behind and a confused situation in his property and estate due to not having an executed will. Even though Henry Springer encountered severe financial difficulties and had overextended himself, he built a business empire.

The Henry Springer property retains most of its original form and is visible from the plaza with minor changes. It was modified during the Puebloization of Old Town in the 1950s as Queen Anne and Pueblo Revival style. The exterior red brick is now stuccoed white with blue detail on the cornice, doors and trim. The exterior portal has been removed. The interior has maintained the old woodwork, including the flooring and ornate fixtures. The property adjoins the Manuel Springer home as one large structure. It is registered as a historic landmark, described as "Queen Anne" by the Historic Landmarks Survey of Albuquerque. It was also listed in the State Register of Cultural Properties as part of Old Albuquerque Historic District in 1979.

Chapter 13

JESUS ROMERO STORE

121 Romero Street NW (James Street)

Andres de Jesus Romero was born on February 8, 1859, in Old Albuquerque, Bernalillo County. He was the son of Manuel Antonio Romero and Maria Clara Aniseta Garcia Romero. Jesus attended the Christian Brothers School in Old Albuquerque and St. Michael's College in Santa Fe in 1875. For years, he lived with his widowed mother. He married Mary Springer, daughter of Henry and Placida Saavedra Springer, on September 18, 1882. Jesus Romero was a prominent merchant, politician, coroner, probate judge and sheriff. He also served as a chair and treasurer of a committee to raise funds for the expansion and repair of San Felipe de Neri Church. While his grocery store was in operation, he held several official Bernalillo County positions through the years, including county coroner (1891), county commissioner (1898), probate judge (1903–9) and sheriff (1909–13).

Jesus built a new building for his grocery store in 1886 on James Street (121 Romero Street NW). The property grounds west from the store once belonged to Henry Springer, owner of Mint Saloon and father-in-law of Jesus Romero. It was the former site of the Central Bank owned by Joshua Raynolds, president, with his brothers Jefferson and Frederick in 1878. The Raynolds brothers were key members of Old and New Albuquerque for financial, insurance and educational institutions. Central Bank moved to New Town Albuquerque at Gold Avenue and Second Street. Today, the building bears the name "Central Bank" on the iron threshold. In 1881, the Central Bank purchased control of the First National Bank of Albuquerque

Above: Central Bank, 1878. *Albuquerque Museum, gift of Byron Johnson PA1978.134.001.*

Left: Jesus Romero store. *Personal collection by Debra Montoya, 2022.*

and First National Bank of El Paso. In 1902, Joshua served as president of Occidental Life Insurance in New Town Albuquerque. From 1913 until his death in 1916, Joshua was president of the Raynolds Addition Company, an Albuquerque real estate development enterprise.

Jesus built his store in the Territorial and Queen Anne style, a combination of adobe with a portico that wraps around the north and east sides, squared posts and milled lumber, plate-glass windows and a corrugated metal roof with irregular profiles. There is a corner gable over the main entrance with a larger gable with scalloped shingles on the east end. The interior has an elaborate stamped metal ceiling and original hardwood floors. It is registered as a historic landmark, described as "Territorial style," by the Historic Landmarks Survey of Albuquerque. It was also listed in the State Register of Cultural Properties as part of the Old Albuquerque Historic District in 1979. On April 26, 2004, for the Tri-Centennial Celebration, Mayor Martin Chavez had a memorial plaque installed on a lamppost in Old Town Plaza honoring Joshua Raynolds as a merchant for contributions to both Old and New Town Albuquerque.

Today, the Jesus Romero store is visible from the plaza as the least altered. It was modified during the Puebloization of Old Town in the 1950s as Territorial and Queen Anne style. The exterior has retained the roof of corrugated metal with the diagonal corner entrance, and the portal appears to be original with the wooden posts. The interior has retained the elaborate stamped metal ceiling. A wood viga ceiling has been added on the expanded portion of the structure. Red brick flooring has been added throughout. The Jesus Romero store is a classic example of commercial style from the 1890s of adobe construction. Through the years, it has housed several businesses, including the ORMSBY Corner, the Color Spot and Pat Read Indian Trader, and it currently operates as the Romero Street Gallery, which has been in operation for forty-three years.

Chapter 14

EL PARRILLAN

201 Romero Street NW (Santiago Street)

Т he building structure known as El Parrillan (open-air market) was originally the site of the home of Santiago and Juliana Hubbell (Ganado, Arizona trading post) in 1867. It was also known as the Sanchez property, owned by Eliseo Sanchez, who owned the land for forty-nine years. In later years, Colonel William McGuiness (born on May 12, 1837, in Dublin, Ireland) occupied the house while he was serving at the army post in Old Albuquerque.

According to *Old Town Albuquerque, New Mexico: A Guide to Its History and Architecture*, "Legend has it that from the steps of this house in 1862, while serving in the Army, he first saw his future wife, then a child, running through falling artillery shells in an attempt to rescue her doll from the family home on the plaza, fearful that the invading confederates would capture it."

William married Leonor Serna, daughter of Pedro Antonio and Manuela Fernandez Serna, in 1865, and together they had a son named Roger McGuinness. William came to the United States at the age of twenty and enlisted in the United States Army. He was ordered to New Mexico to force the Navajo Native American uprising. He later reenlisted and fought in the Civil War on the Federal side. He took part in the Battle of Valverde and other battles between the Federals and Confederates. After the Civil War, he settled in Kansas City, Missouri, only staying there for a brief time before returning to Old Albuquerque and living at the southeast corner of the plaza on Short Street (202 San Felipe Street NW). He conducted a hotel for a brief time. He then engaged in the printing business and published the *Republican*

Above: Santiago Street looking north, circa 1880. *Denver Public Library, Western Collection PA1972.073.001.*

Left: El Parrillan. *Personal collection by Debra Montoya, 2022.*

Review from 1870 to 1876. The paper was published weekly in both English and Spanish and was the only paper published in Old Albuquerque at the time. He also aided the Jesuit fathers, allowing them the use of the paper to serve the San Felipe de Neri parish bulletin. It was during this time that he remarried a second time in 1874, to Encarnacion Romero, daughter of Juan and Victoria Archibeque Romero, and together they had four children.

The original house William occupied was demolished, and the property, built in 1898, was allowed to become a traditional Hispanic-style open-air market. Each morning, activity was busy on the west side of the plaza with fresh meat hung from the porch where women would sit on the ground to sell fresh fruit and vegetables. While the women managed their business, the men were inside the cantina of Don Eliseo Sanchez, where the saloon was adjoining the marketplace. Through the years, it also housed several businesses, including a barbershop. In 1969, a second story was added to the structure with the original design of Territorial trim around the doors and windows. It is registered as a historic landmark, described as Territorial style by the Historic Landmarks Survey of Albuquerque. Today, El Parrillan is visible from the plaza. The second story is harmonious with the original first floor and operates as Mati by Kabana Jewelers.

Chapter 15

JESUS ROMERO HOUSE

205 Romero Street NW (Santiago Street)

Andres de Jesus Romero was born on February 8, 1859, in Old Albuquerque, Bernalillo County. For more background information on Jesus, see chapter 13.

Jesus built a new building for his grocery store in 1886 on James Street (121 Romero Street NW), which was the former site of the Central Bank owned by Joshua Raynolds with his brothers Jefferson and Frederick, the former First National Bank of Albuquerque. In 1915, Jesus built a two-story adobe home with both Prairie and Mediterranean style with a wide roof overhang and a red tile pitched roof with banded windows and an enclosed porch. The home was the last residence erected in Old Albuquerque and has since retained its original residential character on the exterior. The original interior flooring was flat yellow pine except for the dining room. The dining room contained a circular brass plate on the floor that served as a buzzer system to call a servant from the kitchen. The home heating system was steaming radiators in each room.

Jesus Romero was known for his "grand ball parties," including the finest music and dancing. On July 4, 1902, in the Old Town Society Hall, he featured an orchestra with fifty musicians with fellow Old Albuquerque resident Charles Bottger. The funds raised from the ball were used for the "Beautification of the Plaza." Jesus and his wife, Mary, lived in their home until his death on August 16, 1935, at the age of seventy-six. His funeral was a gathering of prominent men in all ranks of politics and citizenship paying tribute to his admirable character. After the death of Jesus Romero,

Top: Zamora store and Romero house on left, 1932. *Albuquerque Museum, gift of Dewey Mann PA2003.008.505.*

Bottom: Jesus Romero house. *Personal collection by Debra Montoya, 2022.*

the street name of his residence was changed to "Romero Street" in his honor. It was previously named "Santiago" for Santiago Baca, son-in-law of Salvador Armijo, Old Albuquerque resident. Mary Romero continued living in the home for a couple of years until she sold it to her sister Luciana in 1937. Unfortunately, Mary passed away on March 5, 1937. In 1943, the home became the Frances Lynn House for unwed mothers.

Today, the Jesus Romero house is visible from the plaza, described as "Prairie and Mediterranean" style. It was not modified during the Puebloization of Old Town in the 1950s and has retained its original character. The exterior has had minor changes with the addition of wrought-iron fencing above the balcony and railing on the front stairs. Red brick has been installed on the outdoor front patio. The interior has had the most changes with upgrades of heating, cooling and electrical system. The wood flooring has been added in two different shades on the lower and upper levels. Carpet has been added on the staircase and upper level. The extension on the rear of the home was added after 1915. It is registered as a historic landmark, described as "Eclectic Adobe" by the Historic Landmarks Survey of Albuquerque. It was also listed in the State Register of Cultural Properties as part of Old Albuquerque Historic District in 1979. On April 26, 2004, for the Tri-Centennial Celebration, Mayor Martin Chavez had a memorial plaque installed on a lamppost in Old Town Plaza honoring Jesus Romero as sheriff and judge. Today, the building is operating as Amapola Gallery, a local artist co-op shop.

Chapter 16

FLORENCIO ZAMORA STORE

301 Romero Street NW (Santiago Street)

F lorencio R. Zamora was born on February 14, 1877, in Old Albuquerque. He was the son of Juan Zamora and Jacobita Romero, who had three children. Florencio married Eligia Duran, born on October 12, 1880, in Old Albuquerque, daughter of Francisco and Concepcion Duran. They were married on March 28, 1895, and had four daughters. Florencio's occupation was a farm laborer in the early 1900s; by 1910, records indicate he was a butcher and owned a "Butcher and Grocery Store" on Santiago Street (301 Romero Street).

The original property grounds were built and owned by Franz Huning to house his mercantile establishment. The former property site also housed the first church, known as San Francisco Xavier, founded by Don Francisco Cuervo y Valdez, who founded the city of Albuquerque. The building was built in 1893, constructed of red pug mill brick, also called fired adobe. The structure is a flat roof, single story, with roof steps down to the rear of the building. It has six-paned large windows beneath segmental arches and elaborate brick work on the cornice. The interior has a high ceiling and hardwood flooring with an open floor plan. In 1913, Florencio sold his business establishment to a former employee, Charles Mann, who also owned the rectangular-shaped adobe building known as a barn to store his equipment and produce.

In later years, Florencio maintained his occupation as a "butcher" but had many legal issues. According to the *Albuquerque Morning Journal* of October

Santiago Street (Romero Street), Florencio Zamora store (post office), circa 1885. *Albuquerque Museum, gift of Center for Southwest Research, University of New Mexico PA1978.050.099.*

22, 1917, "Justo Alderete's suit for $15,000 against Florencio Zamora of Old Albuquerque, is set for trial in the district court today. The suit is an out-come of the shooting of Alderete at Old Albuquerque a year ago. A bullet fired from a rifle struck him in the face, causing an ugly wound. The shooting occurred at night."

On October 24, 1917, according to the *Albuquerque Morning Journal*:

> *Justo Alderete was awarded judgement for $7,500.00 against Florencio Zamora of Old Albuquerque by a jury in the district court yesterday afternoon. The jury took the case at 1:30 o'clock went to lunch because court had continued in session during lunch hour, returned to the courthouse and brought in the verdict shortly after 3:30 o'clock. Alderete charged that Zamora fired a shot which disfigured his face, knocked out his front teeth and broke his lower jaw. Alderete was standing in the rear of a saloon at Old Albuquerque at the time. It was at night, no one saw Zamora fire the shot although circumstantial evidence indicated that he did. He was found guilty of the charge of assault with a deadly weapon, as the result of the shooting at the March term and fined $700.*

Florencio Zamora store and Charles Mann store. *Personal collection by Debra Montoya, 2022.*

Florencio Zamora's other legal issues included cattle stealing, and he was found guilty in district court of larceny of two head cattle on October 11, 1919, according to the *Albuquerque Morning Journal* of October 12. In the 1930s, Florencio bought the former residence of Cristobal Armijo at 2004 South Plaza NW (James Street), known to the locals as La Mansion Historical de Zamora.

Today, the building is visible from the plaza with minor changes. It was changed during the Puebloization of Old Town in the 1950s as Modified Territorial style. Through the years, the interior and exterior have remained intact with minor changes. The exterior red brick has been painted white, and the interior has the original hardwood floors with the same open floor plan. It is registered as a historic landmark, described as "Railroad era Brick" style by the Historic Landmarks Survey of Albuquerque. It was also listed in the State Register of Cultural Properties as part of Old Albuquerque Historic District in 1979. On April 26, 2004, for the Tri-Centennial Celebration, Mayor Martin Chavez had a memorial plaque installed on a lamppost in Old Town Plaza honoring Florencio Zamora as a merchant for his contributions to both Old and New Town Albuquerque.

The former Florencio Zamora store continued operation under new ownership, with Charles Mann operating as postmaster, until 1941. It was one of three stores that existed in early Old Albuquerque. Records indicate

Charles Mann was a farmer, merchant and postmaster for years and successful in his business, also owning the simple adobe barn north of his general store. In later years, it operated as Lutheys Indian Trader and is most known for its years as Old Town Basket and Gift Shop, which unfortunately closed in 2021. A new business opened, and it is now operating as Noisy Water Winery, a franchise company.

Chapter 17

CHARLES MANN BARN AND STORE

309 Romero Street (Santiago Street)/
301 Romero Street (Santiago Street)

C harles Mann was born on April 30, 1863, in Mascoutah, St.
Clair, Illinois. He was the son of John Mann and Martha Boller,
descendants from Germany, who married on September 18, 1859,
in Belleville, St. Clair. Charles married Margarette (Maggie) Bockman, a
descendant from Germany, on May 4, 1888. Margarette was born on May
3, 1873, in Illinois. Charles and Margarette had three children. Charles and
family originally lived in Pueblitos (Valencia County), New Mexico, where
he managed a general merchandise store and Indian trading depot. In 1906,
the family moved to Old Albuquerque, where he worked at the Zamora
Grocery Store owned by Florencio Zamora. Charles soon began purchasing
land to open a market garden. He purchased land with a rectangular-
shaped adobe building with a gabled frame roof that featured a portal to
store equipment and produce on Santiago Street (309 Romero Street). He
purchased the barn from Clara Huning Fergusson, a Huning descendant.
The property grounds were originally part of the Franz Huning mercantile
establishment. The site was also part of the grounds that housed the original
San Felipe Church, rectory and cemetery.

A few years later, as Charles Mann was tearing down an old adobe house,
according to the *Albuquerque Citizen* of December 9, 1908:

> *Workmen who were tearing down an old adobe house adjoining the post
> office in Old Albuquerque yesterday, unearthed a tin, which was imbedded
> in the walls of the structure. The can was found to contain a* Mexico

Press, a newspaper published at Albuquerque, bearing the date of August 30, 1864, a note signed by F. and S. Huning, a one-dollar bill of the date of 1862, which was wrapped around paper bills of the denominations of five, ten, twenty-five and fifty cents. The note was written copy of the New on light, blue ruled paper in a perfectly legible hand, and says: The house where the can was found served both as a residence and store and in it; Franz Huning conducted a store for more than forty years. The ruins of the mill referred to in the note can still be seen on West Central Avenue.

The contents were in the possession of Charles Mann for many years for all to view. Today, the barn is visible from the plaza and intact. It was modified during the Puebloization of Old Town in the 1950s as "Simple Adobe Barn with some Territorial Style trim," with minor changes to the exterior, including added windows with white wood trim, new roof and stucco. The interior still has the remnants of a simple barn, with white painted wood walls, an added staircase and the existing gabled barn roof. It is registered as a historic landmark, described as "Adobe Barn" by the Historic Landmarks Survey of Albuquerque. Documented folklore affirm that the old adobe barn served more as a general store. It housed New Mexico's oldest Summer House Theater, operating with an arena stage. For many years, the barn housed several businesses, including the Summer House Theater, New Vic Players and Casa Talavera. Today, the barn is operating as Oaxacan Zapotec House, owned by Juan Gonzalez, with a new address of 303 Romero Street NW due to the addition of the Plaza Don Luis.

In 1913, Charles purchased another business establishment from his former employer, Florencio Zamora, located on Santiago Street (301 Romero Street) and operated it as a general store and post office until 1941.

Left: Mann farmhouse, 1932. *Albuquerque Museum, gift of Dewey Mann PA2003.008.048.*

Right: Charles Mann barn. *Personal collection by Debra Montoya, 2022.*

It was one of three stores in early Old Albuquerque. Charles also became a landmark when schoolchildren learned of the First Emperor Charlemagne in their history lessons, as they often confused him as a relative. Today, the building is visible from the plaza with minor changes. It was modified during the Puebloization of Old Town in the 1950s as Modified Territorial style. The exterior red brick has been painted white, and the interior has the original hardwood floors with the same open floor plan. It is registered as a historic landmark, described as "Railroad era Brick" style by the Historic Landmarks Survey of Albuquerque. It was also listed in the State Register of Cultural Properties as part of Old Albuquerque Historic District in 1979.

Records indicate Charles Mann was a farmer, merchant and postmaster for years and was successful in his business, also owning the simple adobe barn north of his general store. Charles sold the building in 1941 and moved to National City, California. He died on November 3, 1943. The building operated as Roneys Grocery store until 1958. In the 1950s, neighborhood teenagers would hang out on the south side of the building along the alley after school and carve their names into the red brick along the south side of the building, clearly visible today. In later years, the building operated as a dealer in general merchandise, Lutheys Indian Trader and was most known for years as Old Town Basket and Gift Shop, which unfortunately closed in 2021. A new business opened and is operating as Noisy Water Winery, a franchise company.

Chapter 18

ANTONIO VIGIL HOUSE

413 Romero Street (Santiago Street)

S antiago de Jesus Baca was born on July 25, 1843, in Santa Fe. He was the son of Major Jesus Maria Baca y Salazar and Maria de Jesus Eugenia Salazar, who were married on September 5, 1840. Santiago married Piedad Sarracino y Armijo, daughter of Salvador Armijo, a wealthy rancher and nephew of General Manuel Armijo, and Maria de las Nieves Sarracino de Armijo, daughter of prominent family from the Plaza de Los Padillas, south of Albuquerque. The marriage took place on March 5, 1862, with a wedding ceremony held in San Felipe de Neri Church.

Santiago Baca was educated in the school under charge of Bishop Lamy in Santa Fe. He was known as flamboyant and an entrepreneur in many business and political ventures throughout his life. He started at the early age of seventeen when he was elected chief clerk of the territorial council. He was a businessman; politician; farmer; stock raiser; licensed liquor dealer; sawmill owner in Chilili, New Mexico; land developer (the Baca and Baca/ Armijo additions); and postmaster. He was an enthusiastic horseman and purchased well-bred "American" mares in the East to improve his draft and saddle stock, including an outstanding stallion named Saint Cloud.

In 1864, Salvador, Santiago's father-in-law, admitted him into a partnership doing business as Salvador Armijo y Hijo, with estimated gross receipts of $100,000. The new partnership was aggressive and increased farmland sales by opening branch stores throughout the state. They were also consigning goods to the Native American trading posts in Arizona Territory. In June 1867, they suffered a serious setback when their wagon

Romero Street, with Antonio Vigil house on right, circa 1885. *Albuquerque Museum, gift of Dennis Cummings PA1980.031.001.*

train was attacked by a group of Kiowa, Comanche and Apache Indians and seventy-two mules valued at $200 each and one mare valued at $300 were killed. The incident resulted in a lawsuit filed in the court of claims in Washington, which took over thirty years to settle.

Santiago held several public offices, including legislative council in the town of Pecos, San Miquel County, New Mexico, where he served in the twenty-first legislative assembly in 1873. He also served two terms on the council of Bernalillo County (1878 and 1882). He was president in 1878, in the twenty-third legislative assembly. In Bernalillo County, he served as probate clerk, assessor, sheriff, collector and postmaster in 1877 for four years. Santiago and Piedad moved to Albuquerque from Pecos, New Mexico, in 1874 to facilitate and complete the division of property due to the separation of tangled business assets of his in-laws, Salvador and Maria Nieves Armijo. This was a difficult process that took over ten years to complete with a stipulation agreement in place for their division of business interests, naming Santiago trustee of Maria Nieves's portion. Salvador deeded the home on Main Street (618 Rio Grande Boulevard NW) and a large section of the adjoining orchards, vineyards and farmlands north of Old Albuquerque Plaza to Maria Nieves for $10,000, an extremely large sum for the time. At the same time, Salvador presented deeds to most of his remaining real estate property, including farmland and town lots, to his daughter Piedad and his sister Placida Armijo de Montoya. Piedad received a piece of land north of Old Albuquerque Plaza that her father had purchased in 1869 from Juan Apodaca and Jesus Sanchez for $400. It was situated on a one-hundred-foot-square lot and was the site of an eleven-room house with a plazuela (small square) and zaguan (covered entrance) that adjoined the property that he held to the north.

Santiago, an assertive businessperson, purchased additional lots adjoining the property his wife had received from her father. The combined property faced Main Street, later renamed Santiago in his honor, where he erected three buildings, including the one known as the Antonio Vigil house, built in 1879. The residence was originally built for Albert Grunsfeld, a German merchant, who managed Spiegelberg Brothers, one of the territory's most important general merchandising firms, based in Santa Fe. Grunsfeld moved his family to manage the Spiegelberg branch in Old Albuquerque and became a partner in the enterprise, later joining his brother in buying the remaining Spiegelberg assets. Grunsfeld soon realized that New Town Albuquerque would be the area's future for a commercial center and moved the Spiegelberg store and his residence in 1882. At the same time, he sublet his home to Daniel Geary, cashier and stockholder in the newly organized First National Bank of Albuquerque. Unfortunately, Geary was a poor tenant, leaving Grunsfeld no alternative but to file a suit for damages due to deterioration of the house in April 1885.

The plans for the house were included in an 1879 agreement between Santiago and Albert. It is a one-story flat roofed building with sheet metal (canals) protruding to the east, pine timber simulating vigas with the façade flush with the sidewalk without a setback. It was built with terrones (oversized adobe bricks cut from sod) with twenty-seven-foot-thick walls resting on a stone foundation. The entry is a T-shaped hallway, which provides access to three rooms along the south wall and the double file of rooms to the north. The entrance is off-center toward the south and was originally flanked by three double-hung large windows. The interior walls were eleven feet in height with hard plastered walls, brick floors and corner fireplaces and ceiling tablas (square-shaped boards between the ceiling beams). When the house was built, plans called for a walled placita to the north entered by a zaguan large enough for a wagon. The enclosed area housed a stable, servant quarters and storage areas for firewood and other supplies.

Santiago Baca maintained his business affairs for many years, and anticipating the arrival of the railroad, Old Albuquerque (Old Town

Plaza) had a surge of business activity. He took advantage of the large arrival of merchants, professionals and workers who created the demand for rental property. The demand declined between 1883 and 1885, when New Albuquerque residential suburbs were developed. Santiago opened the first wholesale liquor business establishment in Old Albuquerque, named Dougher & Baca and founded in April 1880. They built the first two-story business house in Old Albuquerque. The business was lucrative, serving many saloons. Santiago later purchased the business in September 1880, with Major Ernest Meyers as manager. The business moved to New Albuquerque in 1881 and was purchased by Lowenthal & Meyers on January 6, 1885. Around the same time, Santiago and Piedad inherited the Maria Nieves home on Main Street NW (618 Rio Grande NW). The same year, he filed a plat on a real estate subdivision west of the railroad tracks near the new depot, named the Baca Addition and Baca and Armijo Additions, located in the Barelas neighborhood spanning from Nicholas Avenue SW to Atlantic Avenue SW. During the next three years, he sold more than 120 lots for over $16,000, and the other real estate sales provided an income of $30,000 from land sales.

Santiago was also active in local politics. A veteran of two sessions in the territorial legislature as a member of the council from San Miquel County, while he lived in Pecos, New Mexico, he was reelected to the same body from Bernalillo County in 1882. Two years later, he was the Republican candidate for county sheriff and tax collector, defeating his wife's cousin Perfecto Armijo. In 1886, he was unable to support the Republican candidate for territorial delegate, who left suddenly, and ran for reelection as a Democrat and then lost to Republican Jose Leandro Perea Jr. After Santiago's loss in 1887, his records were then forwarded to Jose Perea, and it became evident that Santiago's tax accounts were short several thousand dollars, the result of an embezzlement by one of his deputies who had fled the territory. Although the amount involved was not large, there was no attempt to make Santiago criminally liable. This was the beginning of Santiago's financial difficulty with his already strained and heavily mortgaged resources. This led to a financial disaster from which he never recovered. To provide a surety for the loss, Santiago pledged almost all his real property, including the Vigil house, to County Commissioner Mariano S. Otero, the first of a series of trustees.

After six years of litigation, portions of Santiago's holdings were sold at a sheriff's sale held at the front door of the Bernalillo County Courthouse on September 23, 1893, to repay his debts. The highest bidder for all the various pieces of land offered was Baca's daughter Francisca Baca de Chaves, with her husband, Meliton Chaves. This raised sufficient cash to keep the property in the family. She purchased back the Vigil house for $800. In June 1900, the Bacas sold the Antonio Vigil property, and during the next four years, its title changed hands twice more. It was later bought by Pilar Vigil in 1904, whose descendants kept it for years. In 1922, ownership passed to Pilar's son Antonio Vigil, who lived there for almost forty years until his death in 1961. On the east side in the largest room of the structure, he kept the San Felipe Family Grocery Store for many years. During the 1920s, he constructed a small addition to the west, originally used as a garage and chicken house and converted into an apartment.

Santiago de Jesus Baca died on October 23, 1908, listed as a merchant living at 508 West Silver. He was a successful businessperson and held several public offices. A member of the oldest Spanish families in the Rio Grande Valley, he was one of the earliest settlers and most respected citizens of Old Albuquerque. He was known as a fearless sheriff and a trustful officer. He was a factor in business and territorial politics and proved to be a cautious and judicious lawmaker.

Until the death of Antonio Vigil in 1961, the house was used for various commercial purposes and was vacant at one time but remained in the Vigil family. Ray Sandoval, a businessperson who restored the structure for a restaurant-store complex, later leased it. He installed new adobe, colored stucco on exterior and window woodwork with white painted sash trim. The interior was sheetrocked; the drop ceilings were removed, exposing the original beams and boards, including new electrical wiring. It is registered

Antonio Vigil house. *Personal collection by Debra Montoya, 2022.*

as a historic landmark, described as "Territorial" style by the Historic Landmarks Survey of Albuquerque. It was added to the New Mexico State Register of Cultural Properties on July 30, 1976, and the U.S. National Register of Historic Places on May 5, 1978.

Today, the Vigil house is visible from the plaza and is a fine example of construction before the period of the railroad. It was modified during the Puebloization of Old Town in the 1950s as "Territorial and Pueblo Revival." The exterior has been altered with stucco of a modern material and removal of the false pine vigas. The north window (closest to the door) has been replaced by two smaller ones, and all doors and windows are protected with wrought iron. The interior has been altered at various times. The T-shaped entry hallway has been shortened with new doorways installed on the north, south and west. The brick floors appear to be original, but some rooms have been replaced with carpet. It has served as a series of shops, restaurants, galleries and apartments. Today, it is operating as Hidden Gems of the Rio Grande and rental apartments.

Chapter 19

SALVADOR ARMIJO HOUSE

Main Street (618 Rio Grande Boulevard NW)

Salvador Antonio Armijo was born on January 23, 1823, in Old Albuquerque. He was the son of Ambrosio Armijo and Maria Antonia Ortiz, who were married on October 28, 1811, a marriage representing the union of two leading New Mexico families. Salvador was the nephew of General Manuel Armijo, the Mexican governor of New Mexico, who was in command in the territory when the United States acquired the area. The former residence of General Manuel Armijo was a forty-room hacienda located at the corner of Railroad Avenue and Short Street (Central and San Felipe Streets). It was later sold to his nephew Cristobal Armijo, cousin to Salvador.

Salvador Armijo was born into farming, ranching, trading and politics, a powerful background in which he was to assume a position of leadership. He had some education and was literate in both Spanish and English. He acquired knowledge in farming, sheep ranching and freighting as the youngest partner in his family. Early in his career, he engaged in land speculation, buying and selling vineyards and fields between Los Candelarias (north of Old Albuquerque) and Los Barelas (south of Old Albuquerque). He soon started retail merchandising, including freighting and wholesaling ventures, often traveling to Mexican trade centers. In the 1850s, he operated a general store in Old Albuquerque, and soon after, he was a licensed wine merchant.

Salvador had an active role in local politics and civic affairs, following the footsteps of his father and uncles. He held in 1851–52 the office of alcalde (mayor) of Albuquerque, which the Armijos had dominated for thirty years.

Salvador Armijo house. *Personal collection by Debra Montoya, 2022.*

Ten years later, he was elected probate court clerk and in 1867 county treasurer, an office he held for six years. In 1863, he was elected president of the board of aldermen, the body that administered leadership for tough new code ordinances to make the town a desirable place to live. He was elected vice president for the construction of the railroads into New Mexico. He was an encouragement and contributor of the Old Albuquerque early school system, directing Jesuit priests. He provided funding for masses, sermons and processions, particularly during holy week. He was generous with his time and money in promoting programs for New Mexico economic advancement. Salvador married his first cousin Paula Montoya in February 1847. The marriage lasted a year, ending in a separation and divorce in 1848. Shortly after, he began a difficult relationship with Maria Nieves Sarracino, daughter of a prominent family from the Plaza de Los Padillas, south of Albuquerque. She had a daughter, Piedad Armijo, born in 1847.

In 1849, Salvador purchased fifty acres of irrigated farmland north of Old Albuquerque (Old Town Plaza) and a twelve-room house with corrals and buildings from his older brother Jose Armijo y Ortiz, who added his mother's family name to distinguish himself. The construction was typical of nineteenth-century New Mexico architecture, when building materials were scarce and structures were built for defense. It was a flat-roof, one-story dwelling approximately one hundred by seventy feet surrounding a placita (courtyard) with zaguanes (covered entrances) through the north, south and east walls, which gave access to corrals and outside buildings of the hacienda. On the north, stone was used for the thirty-two-inch-thick walls made of adobe bricks laid on the ground without a foundation, which resulted in settling over time. Exterior surfaces were plastered with the traditional mixture of adobe and straw. Windows were few due to defense and the lack of glass. The roof was covered with packed earth and drained by long *canales* (spouts), which extended two to three feet out from the walls. It was divided into twelve rooms, with dirt floors and plastered adobe walls. The interior was dark, sparsely furnished and unattractive to outsiders.

Salvador owned one hundred acres of land (current boundaries of present day include the area of the sawmill district, north to the freeway to Rio Grande Boulevard and south to the plaza) with substantial value of rights to water from the main irrigation ditch on the east boundary of his property. He was the envy of locals with his grapevines, fruit trees and fields plowed for hay and grain. In addition, he also had a pasture of several thousand sheep and large numbers of horses, mules, cattle and oxen for his growing mercantile business.

In later years, Salvador and Maria Nieve's daughter Piedad Armijo married Santiago Baca on March 5, 1862, with a wedding ceremony held in San Felipe de Neri Church. In 1864, Salvador admitted his son-in-law, Santiago, into a partnership, doing business as Salvador Armijo y Hijo, with estimated gross receipts of $100,000. The new partnership was aggressive and increased farmland sales by opening branch stores throughout the state. They were also consigning goods to the Native American trading posts in Arizona territory. In June 1867, they suffered a serious setback when their wagon train was attacked by a group of Kiowa, Comanche and Apache Indians and seventy-two mules valued at $200 each and one mare valued at $300 were killed. The incident resulted in a lawsuit filed in the court of claims in Washington that took over thirty years to settle. While Salvador was away with the mule trains, Maria Nieves managed the home, adjoining farm and ranch enterprise. While in her control, the farmlands were extensively developed, and their value was greatly enhanced by this productivity. By 1860, Salvador had purchased an additional ninety acres for $3,200, adjoining his original fifty-acre home north of Old Albuquerque. The lands were the envy of many, with Salvador becoming the community's wealthiest and most important citizen. According to the federal census report, Salvador was running two hundred cattle and two thousand sheep that was registered a brand with Bernalillo County authorities, one of the first to be recorded. He also maintained a small horse-powered gristmill, one of ten to twelve operating in the country. In 1860, he produced 3,500 pounds of flour and cornmeal; however, all small entrepreneurs were put out of business by large steam-powered mills established by the Huning brothers.

In 1874, Santiago and Piedad moved to Old Albuquerque to live with Maria Nieves until her death on April 13, 1898, to facilitate and complete the division of property due to the separation of tangled business assets of his in-laws, Salvador and Maria Nieves Armijo, a process that took over ten years to complete. A stipulation agreement was in place for their division of business interests, naming Santiago trustee of Maria Nieves's portion. Salvador deeded the twelve-room house on Main Street (618 Rio Grande Boulevard NW), corrals, outside buildings and large section of the adjoining orchards, vineyards and farmlands north of Old Albuquerque Plaza to Maria Nieves for $10,000, an extremely considerable sum for the time. At the same time, Salvador presented deeds to most of his remaining real estate property, including farmland and town lots, to his daughter Piedad and his sister Placida Armijo de Montoya. He retained only his lands at Los Duranes and Ranchos de Atrisco. The latter property was sold in March 1876 to relative Jesus Armijo with the notation in the deed that $1,650 was still due to Maria Nieves.

At the same time, Salvador began reinvesting in similar properties at Ranchos de Atrisco (west of the Rio Grande), Las Lagunitas (south of Barelas), Los Duranes (north of Old Albuquerque), San Antonio, Tijeras and Canoncito de Nuanes in the east mountains of Albuquerque. He also acquired a location near Old Albuquerque for warehouses and living quarters. The census of 1870 shows he was the largest farmer in Old Albuquerque with three hundred acres under cultivation, with his lands producing wheat, corn and beans. He was also the community's largest agricultural employer, with an annual payroll exceeding $4,000. That same year, he also had an increased number of sheep from two thousand to six thousand, and the price of wool increased from four cents to eighteen cents a pound in 1871. Salvador started over, leaving Albuquerque to live in Peralta, New Mexico, and surprvise his Valencia County store, where he opened a hotel and "traveler's rest." He later remarried twenty-eight-year-old Maria Candelaria de la Trinidad Candelaria Ortiz on August 19, 1875. Three years later, in 1878, Salvador returned to Albuquerque and began building an elaborate house on his property at Los Duranes with ample facilities for entertaining. He opened a store in Old Albuquerque Plaza across from the Centennial Hotel and began to reestablish himself in the ewe livestock business. In the spring of 1879, while in Arizona looking after his livestock, he was ill and taken to the house of Juliana Garcia de Sedillo in El Arroyo Carrizo, north of St. Johns, where he lingered for two weeks. On April 4, 1879, he died. His last act that was mentioned was to deed the new house in Los Duranes and tract of farmland described as *tierra rica* (rich land) to his spouse and children. As soon as the news reached Albuquerque, Jose Armijo y Ortiz, brother of Salvador, hired a wagon and four men to haul a casket and monument over the long trail to Arizona to bury his brother.

After the sudden death of Salvador, with no will left and affairs confused, his widow and Nestor Montoya, his former brother-in-law, were named his executors, but they declined to serve. Jesus Maria Perea was named administrator by Bernalillo County probate judge Justo R. Armijo, a distant cousin of Salvador's. The settlement of the estate involved taking inventory and selling all of Salvador's remaining goods and livestock, collecting outstanding obligations and paying off many creditors. The debts of the estate would have exceeded its assets. There was an attempt to take over some of the land given to his daughter Piedad and his sister Placida, but this was later blocked by a legal action from Santiago Baca, son-in-law, and resulted in the matter of his estate remaining unresolved. Shortly before the turn of the century, the federal government settled the claims for Native American depredations that had been pending for over thirty years. Immediately, Maria, Salvador's ex-widow, and Santiago, his son-in-law, entered a court battle over the administration of the Salvador Armijo estate.

The Armijo family is significant to the history in Old Albuquerque (Old Town Plaza) as original early settlers and a prominent and respectable family in the territory. Today, the former Salvador Armijo home is visible on the north edge of historic Old Town Plaza. It has retained some of its basic original appearance. The residence construction in the 1840s shows the status of wealth for its time. It was built in the closing years of Mexico's control of New Mexico. Its design was common during the Mexican rule in the era for possible Native American attacks. Since its construction in the nineteenth century, it has been refurbished significantly, with each owner making additions and removing sections. It has remained in the Armijo family for five generations. The 1875 remodeling enclosed the zaguanes to form hallways and added new portales, windows with Territorial-style wooden trim. In the early 1900s, most of the west side of the house was demolished, and a new addition was built on the south side. New portals, pitched roofs with ornamental pediments and a cast stone veneer (now removed) were also added to the exterior. Armijo's great-granddaughter Soledad Chacon, New Mexico secretary of state, was a resident in the early 1900s. During the mid-twentieth century, it was converted into apartments. In 1977, Armijo's great-great-granddaughter Frances Wilson sold the house, and it was later turned into a restaurant named Maria Theresa, operating until 2004. In 2009, the former residence was purchased by the adjoining Hotel Albuquerque and turned into a party venue as a nightclub named Casa Esencia.

It was listed in the New Mexico State Register of Cultural Properties on June 20, 1975, and the National Register of Historic Places on October 8, 1976. It is also registered as a historic landmark, described as "Mexican Period Hacienda with Territorial Remodeling" style by the Historic Landmarks Survey of Albuquerque.

Chapter 20

TERRITORIAL FAIR

The first territorial fair (1881–1910) was held on October 3–8, 1881, west of the Old Town Plaza at the southwest corner of Railroad Avenue (Central Avenue) and Main Street (Rio Grande Boulevard), where Walgreens is currently located. It continued west and south on a designated location of twenty acres of land with a racetrack and grandstand. Governor Lionel Sheldon officially opened the fair with the theme "The Civilization of the Nineteenth Century and Civilization of Prehistoric Times," with Elias S. Stover serving as president and Franz Huning as vice president. Others with the same titles over the years were Jose L. Perea, Ambrosio Armijo, M.S. Otero and Thomas D. Post. W.D. Patton was elected secretary for one year, Major H.R. Whiting was chosen as corresponding secretary for one year and W.K.P. Wilson was treasurer. The Executive Committee consisted of Judge William Hazeldine, Santiago Baca, Nicolas T. Armijo, Thomas Hughes and Elwood Madden serving for one year. The New Mexico Agricultural, Mineral and Industrial Exposition and Driving Park Association's purpose was to hold territorial fairs in Albuquerque yearly.

The first exhibition was a modest gathering with minerals and agricultural, pastoral, horticultural and industrial products of the territory in New Mexico. Tents housed such exhibits as fruit, grain, vegetables, saddles, furniture, flowers, textiles, tobacco products, minerals, general merchandise and taxidermy. The racetrack offered horse, mule and foot races, with horses brought in from the West and East Coasts. Cattle arrived from Kansas and Texas and sheep from New Mexico. Stalls for horses and

The entrance to the International Industrial Exposition, 1908 (present-day Central Avenue and Rio Grande Boulevard). *Albuquerque Museum, gift of Grace Miller-Redd PA1993.018.004.*

cattle and pens for sheep and hogs were given for free during the week of the exhibition, with grain, hay and straw furnished at cost if bought at the fairgrounds. There were trotting and running exhibitions and trails for speed. Native American dances were performed by the Pueblos and other tribes with displays of Native American pottery, advertised as "relics from cities of the Montezuma's." The operating hotels at that time advertised for accommodations, and the railroad reduced rates for travel. The prices of admission were a four-horse vehicle for one dollar, two four-horse vehicles for seventy-five cents each, a one-horse vehicle for fifty cents and a two-horse vehicle for twenty-five cents. Admitting ticket prices for one person to enter once, whether on horse, vehicle or by foot, was fifty cents, with children over five and under twelve years of age costing twenty-five cents. Exhibitors' tickets were good for the entire day at the cost of twenty-five cents.

The fair was an immediate success, as recorded by Father Tromby of San Felipe de Neri Church in his Latin history, according to Steele's *Works and Days*:

Fair Held in Albuquerque—Before moving on to our consideration of the affairs of San Felipe Residence, we may be allowed a brief mention of the great Fair held in that town, in which the more noteworthy and excellent items of the whole Territory of New Mexico (those which concern either the fine arts or the riches inherent in the earth) might be seen collected in one place; for the Fair was truly so fine that I would in no wise call it unworthy of the greatest cities. I shall mention nothing of the games and spectacles offered to the populace on that occasion; but the abundance and variety of the metals with which the mines of New Mexico abound were worthy of highest commendation, as was the great concourse of visitors coming from the various states of the Federal Republic.

Unfortunately, a heavy rainstorm continued daily, and most of the horse races, footraces and band concerts were canceled. The fair officials extended the event for another three days for weather to clear, but it continued raining. Attendance was good, but receipts fell short, with boosters having to raise another $1,000 to cover expenses. Overall, the outcome was that all were very satisfied with the event.

The following year, the second fair took place on September 18–23, 1882, with the biggest attractions including the first known professional baseball team in Albuquerque. The first baseball team, known as the Albuquerque Browns, was founded in 1880 by W.T McCreight. They played on the inside running track facing the grandstands at the fairgrounds. McCreight would entice pro players from leagues to play for him for $100 plus expenses. Another huge attraction at the fair that year was the first balloon flight by Professor Park Van Tassel, who ascended from a vacant lot and reached an altitude of 14,207 feet before landing in an Old Town cornfield. The balloon was named "City of Albuquerque." The fair held many special events to attract crowds, including a circus and a four-mile foot race by Zuni runners. Other events included horse and harness racing, bicycle and burro racing, a cakewalk, dancing contests and Native American dances. The second year had many more additions to the existing exhibits, including the Jesuits' booth, which they decorated. B. Moses was known as the cigar man for his fine display of exclusive cigars from cheap to expensive, including a box of Havanas worth $50, as well as beautiful Navajo blankets with beautiful and attractive designs, moccasins, leggings and bows and arrows of fine Native American workmanship. Another fine exhibit was the Spiegelberg Bros. display, catering to women as a temple of fashion, with elegant dresses imported from Paris, including

Albuquerque Browns baseball team, 1893. *Albuquerque Museum, transfer from Albuquerque Public Library PA1978.141.307.*

The balloon ascension of Park Van Tassel, July 4, 1882. *Albuquerque Museum, gift of Center for Southwest Research, University of New Mexico PA1978.050.036.*

a wedding gown of French silk trimmed with beaded Spanish lace and adorned with leaves and flowers of beads valued at $225.

The third fair took place on October 1–6, 1893, with the officers designating a day when all the Catholic schoolchildren in the city were admitted free. Two years later, after the students had enjoyed their free admission, they reciprocated by creating a float that represented the Sisters of Charity schools in the fair parade. As the years passed, special attractions became more elaborate, including an exotic dancer with the Famous Dance of the Pyramids in 1899. In 1903, promoter D.K.B. Sellers organized a mock battle between Navajos and a troop of U.S. cavalry, but the performance was called off when Sellers learned the Navajos had removed the blanks from their guns and replaced them with live ammunition. In 1907, Joseph Blondin flew his balloon filled with coal gas eighteen miles north, but angry farmers fired at the balloon. In 1909, he tried again with no success with his balloon tethered. In 1911, Charles F. Walsh lifted off in a Curtiss biplane from the infield of the track of the fairgrounds and flew south to the Barelas Bridge, then east to the railroad tracks and northwest across Robinson Park. He landed again on the fair track as the first air flight to take place in New Mexico.

Charles Walsh and Roy Stamm preparing to take flight at Territorial Fairgrounds, 1911. *Albuquerque Museum, gift of George Pearl PA1978.001.013.*

In 1908, a huge national and political event took place when local promoters staged an event in conjunction with the Territorial Fair and the Irrigation Congress to host the sixteenth annual International Industrial Exposition. The Irrigation Congress was the nation's most prominent water organization and was pushing for federal funding with multiple water projects in the territory. Albuquerque received plenty of publicity and went all out, erecting an archway entrance at the north corner of Main Street (Rio Grande Boulevard) and Railroad Avenue (Central Avenue). The fair also featured an imitation pueblo designed by University of New Mexico president William G. Tight, who wanted to remodel the university campus in the same style. When the archway structure was torn down in 1910, the material used to build the archway was reused to build two homes south where the county jail was moved to the corner of Main Street and Railroad Avenue. The present homes are on the corner of Rio Grande Boulevard and Merritt Avenue on the south side of street. The street originally known as Roslington Road was changed to Merritt Avenue after John Merritt, who with his family occupied one of the homes and aided in tearing down the archway. The other home was occupied by Joe and Minnie Miller and their children.

The territorial fair reached its peak at the turn of the century, attracting visitors from Arizona, Colorado and Texas until 1910. It became a state fair in 1911 in anticipation of New Mexico's upcoming statehood. The original fairgrounds, known as Traction Park, was used until 1916. Albuquerque Traction Company, operator of the city's electric streetcar, acquired the park, renovated the track, built a casino and added exhibition halls. In 1917, the fair was canceled due to the United States' entry into World War I, and it did not take place for many years. The new fairgrounds was built in 1936–38 with Works Progress Administration funding, which was secured by the efforts of Governor Clyde Tingley. The first fair known as the New Mexico State Fair took place in 1938 with sixty-four thousand visitors at its current location on Central Avenue in the International District.

REFERENCES

Old Town Plaza

Albuquerque City Directory, 1883. R917.8961. Special Collections, Albuquerque/Bernalillo County Library, Albuquerque, New Mexico.

Albuquerque Museum of Art and History.

Albuquerque Tribune, June 24, 1975. Special Collections, Albuquerque/Bernalillo County Library, Albuquerque, New Mexico.

Dewitt, Susan. *Historic Albuquerque Today: An Overview Survey of Historic Buildings and Districts*. 2nd ed. A publication of the Historic Landmarks Survey of Albuquerque. Albuquerque, NM, September 1978.

Fergusson, Erna. "Do You Remember." A series of articles on Old Albuquerque printed in the *Albuquerque Herald*, 1922–23. Special Collections, Albuquerque/Bernalillo County Library, Albuquerque, New Mexico, November 2002.

Steele, Thomas J. *Works and Days: A History of San Felipe Neri Church, 1867–1895*. Albuquerque, NM: Albuquerque Museum, 1983.

San Felipe de Neri Church

Albuquerque City Directory, 1883. R917.8961. Special Collections, Albuquerque/Bernalillo County Library, Albuquerque, New Mexico.

Dewitt, Susan. *Historic Albuquerque Today: An Overview Survey of Historic Buildings and Districts.* 2nd ed. A publication of the Historic Landmarks Survey of Albuquerque. Albuquerque, NM, September 1978.

Greenleaf, Richard. "The Founding of Albuquerque, 1706: An Historical Problem." *New Mexico Historical Review.* Special Collections, Albuquerque/Bernalillo County Library.

Johnson, Byron. *Old Town, Albuquerque, New Mexico: A Guide to Its History and Architecture.* Special Collections, Albuquerque/Bernalillo County Library.

Steele, Thomas J. *Works and Days: A History of San Felipe Neri Church, 1867–1895.* Albuquerque, NM: Albuquerque Museum, 1983.

San Felipe de Neri Rectory

Dewitt, Susan. *Historic Albuquerque Today: An Overview Survey of Historic Buildings and Districts.* 2nd ed. A publication of the Historic Landmarks Survey of Albuquerque. Albuquerque, NM, September 1978.

Johnson, Byron. *Old Town, Albuquerque, New Mexico: A Guide to Its History and Architecture.* Special Collections, Albuquerque/Bernalillo County Library.

Steele, Thomas J. *Works and Days: A History of San Felipe Neri Church, 1867–1895.* Albuquerque, NM: Albuquerque Museum, 1983.

Our Lady of the Angels School/Sister Blandina Convent

Albuquerque Tricentennial. "U.S. Territorial Education, 1846–1912." albuqhistsoc.org/SecondSite/pkfiles/pk117territoreducat.htm

Archdiocese of Santa Fe Office of Communications/Media. www.archdiosf.org.

Dewitt, Susan. *Historic Albuquerque Today: An Overview Survey of Historic Buildings and Districts.* 2nd ed. A publication of the Historic Landmarks Survey of Albuquerque. Albuquerque, NM, September 1978.

Emmer, Regina. "Our Lady of the Angels School." SAH Archipedia. sah-archipedia.org/buildings/NM-01-001-0111-01.

Johnson, Byron. *Old Town, Albuquerque, New Mexico: A Guide to Its History and Architecture.* Special Collections, Albuquerque/Bernalillo County Library.

Our Lady of the Angels/San Felipe (Duranes/Barelas). Albuquerque, NM, San Felipe de Neri Gift Shop pamphlet.

Segale, Sister Blandina, SC. *At the End of the Santa Fe Trail*. N.p.: Sisters of Charity of Cincinnati, 2014.

Steele, Thomas J. *Works and Days: A History of San Felipe Neri Church, 1867–1895*. Albuquerque, NM: Albuquerque Museum, 1983.

Vinegar, Tom. *A Walk Around Old Town*. Albuquerque, NM: Vinegar Tom Press, 1970. Special Collections, Albuquerque/Bernalillo County Library.

Jacob Stueckel House

Albuquerque Journal. "Historic Old Town Plaza Buildings Home for Shopkeepers, Craftsmen." January 3, 1956. Special Collections, Albuquerque/Bernalillo County Library.

———. June 26, 1944. Obituary Index.

Albuquerque Museum. *Old Town: A Walking Tour of History and Architecture*. July 12, 1982. Special Collections, Albuquerque/Bernalillo County Library.

Dewitt, Susan. *Historic Albuquerque Today: An Overview Survey of Historic Buildings and Districts*. 2nd ed. A publication of the Historic Landmarks Survey of Albuquerque. Albuquerque, NM, September 1978.

Palmer, Mo. *Albuquerque Then and Now*. New York: HarperCollins, 2019.

Vinegar, Tom. *A Walk Around Old Town*. Albuquerque, NM: Vinegar Tom Press, 1970. Special Collections, Albuquerque/Bernalillo County Library.

Herman Blueher House

Albuquerque Journal, August 6, 1899. Special Collections, Albuquerque/Bernalillo County Library.

Albuquerque Museum. *Old Town: A Walking Tour of History and Architecture*. July 12, 1982. Special Collections, Albuquerque/Bernalillo County Library.

Albuquerque Tribune, January 12, 1965. Special Collections, Albuquerque/Bernalillo County Library.

Bryan, Howard. "Off the Beaten Path." August 1, 1963. Special Collections, Albuquerque/Bernalillo County Library.

Carlson, Paul, and Geraldine Snow. "A Genealogical Walking Tour of Old Town." Albuquerque Museum, presented for the New Mexico Genealogical Society, October 17, 1987.

Dewitt, Susan. *Historic Albuquerque Today: An Overview Survey of Historic Buildings and Districts.* 2nd ed. A publication of the Historic Landmarks Survey of Albuquerque. Albuquerque, NM, September 1978.

Emmer, Regina. "Hacienda Del Rio Restaurant." SAH Archipedia. sah-archipedia.org/buildings/NM-01-001-0111-07.

Fergusson, Erna. "Old Albuquerque." *Albuquerque Herald*, 1922–23. The First Public School, Albuquerque Public Library, Special Collections, Albuquerque/Bernalillo County Library.

Fisher, Irene. "Old Albuquerque Past Present." Old Albuquerque Historical Society. Special Collections, Albuquerque/Bernalillo County Library.

Franczyk, Jean. "Old Town Tour Voyage to Past." *Albuquerque Journal*, July 3, 1982. Special Collections, Albuquerque/Bernalillo County Library.

Genealogy Trails. "Bernalillo County, New Mexico: Biographies." genealogytrails.com/newmex/bernalillo/biographies.html.

Johnson, Byron, and Robert Dauner. *Early Albuquerque: A Photographic History.* A joint project of the *Albuquerque Journal*, January 1, 1981.

Polston, Cody. *Ghosts of Old Town Albuquerque.* Charleston, SC: The History Press, 2012.

Rebord, Bernice. *A Social History of Albuquerque, 1880–1885.* Albuquerque: University of New Mexico, 1947. Special Collections, Albuquerque/Bernalillo County Library.

Rosales, Andres. "Historic Hacienda del Rio Cantina." haciendadelriocantina.com/our-story.

Stanley, F. *The Duke City: The Story of Albuquerque, New Mexico, 1706–1956.* 1963. Special Collections, Albuquerque/Bernalillo County Library.

Steele, Thomas J. *Works and Days: A History of San Felipe Neri Church, 1867–1895.* Albuquerque, NM: Albuquerque Museum, 1983.

Wikipedia. "Albuquerque High School." en.wikipedia.org/wiki/Albuquerque_High School.

Ambrosio Armijo House

Albuquerque Tribune. "La Placita Plaque Will Be Dedicated at Old Town Fete." May 13, 1972.

American History and Genealogy Project. *History of New Mexico: Its Resources and People.* Vol. 2. Pacific States Publishing Co., 1907. nmahgp.genealogyvillage.com.

Carlson, Paul, and Geraldine Snow. "A Genealogical Walking Tour of Old Town." Albuquerque Museum, presented for the New Mexico Genealogical Society, October 17, 1987.

Dewitt, Susan. *Historic Albuquerque Today: An Overview Survey of Historic Buildings and Districts.* 2nd ed. A publication of the Historic Landmarks Survey of Albuquerque. Albuquerque, NM, September 1978.

Emmer, Regina. SAH Archipedia. "La Placita Dining Rooms." sah-archipedia.org/buildings/NM-01-001-0111-02.

Find a Grave. "Ambrosio Armijo (1817–1882)." www.findagrave.com/memorial/26928278/ambrosio-armijo.

Fisher, Irene. "Old Albuquerque Past Present." Old Albuquerque Historical Society. Special Collections, Albuquerque/Bernalillo County Library.

Johnson, Byron. *Old Town, Albuquerque, New Mexico: A Guide to Its History and Architecture.* Special Collections, Albuquerque/Bernalillo County Library.

Los Poblanos Historic Inn & Organic Farm. "History." lospoblanos.com/about/history.

Palmer, Mo. *Albuquerque Then and Now.* New York: HarperCollins, 2019.

Peterson, Lorraine, UNM journalism student. *Albuquerque Journal*, 1958.

Santa Fe New Mexican, August 11, 1883, 4.

Santa Fe Weekly Gazette, September 24, 1853, image 2.

Segale, Sister Blandina, SC. *At the End of the Santa Fe Trail.* N.p.: Sisters of Charity of Cincinnati, 2014.

Simmons, Marc. *Albuquerque: A Narrative History.* Albuquerque: University of New Mexico Press, n.d., 203–4.

Steele, Thomas J. *Works and Days: A History of San Felipe Neri Church, 1867–1895.* Albuquerque, NM: Albuquerque Museum, 1983.

Stevens, Franchesca, public information specialist with Bernalillo County. Historical Perspective, Court of Wills, Estates and Probate, September 14, 2012.

Charles Bottger House

Arlington National Cemetery. "General Philip H. Sheridan Memorial Grave." www.arlingtoncemetery.mil/Explore/Monuments-and-Memorials/Sheridan-Memorial.

Bauer, W.E. The Public Library Albuquerque and Bernalillo County. "Birthplace of Mrs. Phil Sheridan, Albuquerque, New Mexico." abqlibrary.org/postcards/oldtown.

Bottger Mansion. "History of Bottger Mansion." bottger.com/bottger-mansion-history.

Bryan, Howard. "Off the Beaten Path: Albuquerque's Old Town Plaza." *Albuquerque Tribune*, November 22, 1962.

———. "Off the Beaten Path: Mrs. Emma Yott." *Albuquerque Tribune*, November 18, 1954.

———. "Off the Beaten Path: Sunny Side Inn Proprietor." *Albuquerque Tribune*, June 25, 1964.

Dewitt, Susan. *Historic Albuquerque Today: An Overview Survey of Historic Buildings and Districts*. 2nd ed. A publication of the Historic Landmarks Survey of Albuquerque. Albuquerque, NM, September 1978.

Johnson, Byron. *Old Town, Albuquerque, New Mexico: A Guide to Its History and Architecture*. Special Collections, Albuquerque/Bernalillo County Library.

Johnson, Byron, and Robert Dauner. *Early Albuquerque: A Photographic History*. A joint project of the *Albuquerque Journal*, January 1, 1981.

Rebord, Bernice. *A Social History of Albuquerque, 1880–1885*. Albuquerque: University of New Mexico, 1947. Special Collections, Albuquerque/Bernalillo County Library.

Segale, Sister Blandina, SC. *At the End of the Santa Fe Trail*. N.p.: Sisters of Charity of Cincinnati, 2014.

Vinegar, Tom. *A Walk Around Old Town*. Albuquerque, NM: Vinegar Tom Press, 1970. Special Collections, Albuquerque/Bernalillo County Library.

Whiting, R.H., Albuquerque citizen. December 2, 1908, Chronicling America Historic American Newspapers.

Wikipedia. "Charles A. Bottger House." en.wikipedia.org/wiki/Charles_A._Bottger_House.

Cristobal Armijo House

American History and Genealogy Project. *History of New Mexico: Its Resources and People*. Vol. 2. Pacific States Publishing Co., 1907. nmahgp.genealogyvillage.com.

Dewitt, Susan. *Historic Albuquerque Today: An Overview Survey of Historic Buildings and Districts*. 2nd ed. A publication of the Historic Landmarks Survey of Albuquerque. Albuquerque, NM, September 1978.

———. "La Hacienda Restaurant." SAH Archipedia. sah-archipedia.org/buildings/nm-01-001-0111-03.

Find a Grave. "Capt Juan Cristobal Armijo (1810–1884)." www.findagrave.com/memorial/26930072/juan-cristobal-armijo.

Fisher, Irene. "Old Albuquerque Past Present." Old Albuquerque Historical Society. Special Collections, Albuquerque/Bernalillo County Library.

Genealogy Trails. "Bernalillo County, New Mexico: Biographies." genealogytrails.com/newmex/bernalillo/biographies.html.

Johnson, Byron. *Old Town, Albuquerque, New Mexico: A Guide to Its History and Architecture.* Special Collections, Albuquerque/Bernalillo County Library.

Los Poblanos Historic Inn & Organic Farm. "History." lospoblanos.com/about/history.

Polston, Cody. *Ghosts of Old Town Albuquerque.* Charleston, SC: The History Press, 2012.

Sanborn Fire Insurance Map from Albuquerque, Bernalillo County, New Mexico, 1891, 1893, 1898.

Santa Fe New Mexican, February 18, 1901.

Vinegar, Tom. *A Walk Around Old Town.* Albuquerque, NM: Vinegar Tom Press, 1970. Special Collections, Albuquerque/Bernalillo County Library.

Manuel Springer House

Albuquerque Morning Journal, November 15, 1917.

American History and Genealogy Project. *History of New Mexico: Its Resources and People.* Vol. 2. Pacific States Publishing Co., 1907. nmahgp.genealogyvillage.com.

Carlson, Paul, and Geraldine Snow. "A Genealogical Walking Tour of Old Town." Albuquerque Museum, presented for the New Mexico Genealogical Society, October 17, 1987.

Dewitt, Susan. *Historic Albuquerque Today: An Overview Survey of Historic Buildings and Districts.* 2nd ed. A publication of the Historic Landmarks Survey of Albuquerque. Albuquerque, NM, September 1978.

Emmer, Regina. SAH Archipedia. "The Covered Wagon (Manuel Springer House)." sah-archipedia.org/buildings/NM-01-001-0111-08.

Fisher, Irene. "Old Albuquerque Past Present." Old Albuquerque Historical Society. Special Collections, Albuquerque/Bernalillo County Library.

Johnson, Byron. *Old Town, Albuquerque, New Mexico: A Guide to Its History and Architecture.* Special Collections, Albuquerque/Bernalillo County Library.

NMAHGP. "Manuel R. Springer, Bernalillo County, New Mexico." nmahgp. genealogyvillage.com/cty/manuel_r_springer_bernalillo_county_new_ mexico.html.

Stanley, F. *The Duke City: The Story of Albuquerque, New Mexico, 1706–1956.* 1963. Special Collections, Albuquerque/Bernalillo County Library.

Henry Springer Store

Bryan, Howard. "Off the Beaten Path." November 22, 1962. Special Collections, Albuquerque/Bernalillo County Library.

Carlson, Paul, and Geraldine Snow. "A Genealogical Walking Tour of Old Town." Albuquerque Museum, presented for the New Mexico Genealogical Society, October 17, 1987.

Dewitt, Susan. *Historic Albuquerque Today: An Overview Survey of Historic Buildings and Districts.* 2nd ed. A publication of the Historic Landmarks Survey of Albuquerque. Albuquerque, NM, September 1978.

Emmer, Regina. SAH Archipedia. "The Covered Wagon (Henry Springer Store)." sah-archipedia.org/buildings/NM-01-001-0111-04.

Find a Grave. "Placida Maria Saavedra Springer." www.findagrave.com/ memorial/60240196/placida-maria-springer.

Grace, Mike. "Henry Springer: The Naming of a Town." www.roundvalleyaz. com/springer.html.

Jaramillo, Prospero. "Los Ancianos Hablan: Memorias of Old Town, La Herencia del Norte." Summer 1999. Special Collections, Albuquerque/ Bernalillo County Library.

Johnson, Byron. *Old Town, Albuquerque, New Mexico: A Guide to Its History and Architecture.* Special Collections, Albuquerque/Bernalillo County Library.

Marriages Book "C" and "D," January 1855–December 14, 1900. San Felipe de Neri RCC. Albuquerque Territory of NM, Microfilm FHL 016-644. Special Collections, Albuquerque/Bernalillo County Library.

Sanborn Fire Insurance Map from Albuquerque, Bernalillo County, NM, Library of Congress. www.loc.gov/resource.

Wikipedia. "Springerville, Arizona." en.wikipedia.org/wiki/Springerville,_ Arizona.

Jesus Romero Store

Dewitt, Susan. *Historic Albuquerque Today: An Overview Survey of Historic Buildings and Districts.* 2nd ed. A publication of the Historic Landmarks Survey of Albuquerque. Albuquerque, NM, September 1978.

Emmer, Regina. SAH Archipedia. "Romero Street Gallery (Jesus Romero Store)." sah-archipedia.org/buildings/NM-01-001-0111-05.

Fergusson, Erna. "Old Albuquerque." *Albuquerque Herald,* 1922–23. The First Public School, Albuquerque Public Library, Special Collections, Albuquerque/Bernalillo County Library.

Find a Grave. "Jesus Romero." www.findagrave.com/memorial/60244297/jesus-romero.

From the guide to the Raynolds Family Papers, 1886–1918. University of New Mexico, Center for Southwest Research.

Johnson, Byron. *Old Town, Albuquerque, New Mexico: A Guide to Its History and Architecture.* Special Collections, Albuquerque/Bernalillo County Library.

Johnson, Byron, and Robert Dauner. *Early Albuquerque: A Photographic History.* A joint project of the *Albuquerque Journal,* January 1, 1981.

Rebord, Bernice. *A Social History of Albuquerque, 1880–1885.* Albuquerque: University of New Mexico, 1947. Special Collections, Albuquerque/Bernalillo County Library.

El Parrillan

Dewitt, Susan. *Historic Albuquerque Today: An Overview Survey of Historic Buildings and Districts.* 2nd ed. A publication of the Historic Landmarks Survey of Albuquerque. Albuquerque, NM, September 1978.

Find a Grave. "William McGuinness." www.findagrave.com/memorial/65249524/william-mcguinness.

Johnson, Byron. *Old Town, Albuquerque, New Mexico: A Guide to Its History and Architecture.* Special Collections, Albuquerque/Bernalillo County Library.

Sanchez, Father Robert. *San Felipe de Neri.* Pamphlet, Albuquerque, NM.

Steele, Thomas J. *Works and Days: A History of San Felipe Neri Church, 1867–1895.* Albuquerque, NM: Albuquerque Museum, 1983.

United States Census, 1870.

Vinegar, Tom. *A Walk Around Old Town.* Albuquerque, NM: Vinegar Tom Press, 1970. Special Collections, Albuquerque/Bernalillo County Library.

Jesus Romero House

Carlson, Paul, and Geraldine Snow. "A Genealogical Walking Tour of Old Town." Albuquerque Museum, presented for the New Mexico Genealogical Society, October 17, 1987.

Dewitt, Susan. *Historic Albuquerque Today: An Overview Survey of Historic Buildings and Districts*. 2nd ed. A publication of the Historic Landmarks Survey of Albuquerque. Albuquerque, NM, September 1978.

Emmer, Regina. SAH Archipedia. "Romero House (Jesus Romero House)." sah-archipedia.org/buildings/NM-01-001-0111-09.

Find a Grave. "Jesus Romero." www.findagrave.com/memorial/60244297/jesus-romero.

History of Ownership. Albuquerque Public Library, Specials Collections Document in folder labeled "New Mexico–Bernalillo–Albuquerque–Old Town" as Frances Lynn Home in 1969.

Johnson, Byron. *Old Town, Albuquerque, New Mexico: A Guide to Its History and Architecture*. Special Collections, Albuquerque/Bernalillo County Library.

Florencio Zamora Store

Albuquerque Morning Journal, October 25, 1917; October 12, 1919. Chronicling America, Library of Congress.

Albuquerque Museum. *Old Town: A Walking Tour of History and Architecture*. July 12, 1982. Special Collections, Albuquerque/Bernalillo County Library.

Carlson, Paul, and Geraldine Snow. "A Genealogical Walking Tour of Old Town." Albuquerque Museum, presented for the New Mexico Genealogical Society, October 17, 1987.

Dewitt, Susan. *Historic Albuquerque Today: An Overview Survey of Historic Buildings and Districts*. 2nd ed. A publication of the Historic Landmarks Survey of Albuquerque. Albuquerque, NM, September 1978.

Emmer, Regina. SAH Archipedia. "Basket Shop (Florencio Zamora Store; Charles Mann Store)." sah-archipedia.org/buildings/NM-01-001-0111-06.

Evening Herald, September 18, 1920. Chronicling America, Library of Congress.

Fisher, Irene. "Old Albuquerque Past Present." Old Albuquerque Historical Society. Special Collections, Albuquerque/Bernalillo County Library.

Jaramillo, Prospero. "Los Ancianos Hablan: Memorias of Old Town, La Herencia del Norte." Summer 1999. Special Collections, Albuquerque/Bernalillo County Library.

Johnson, Byron. *Old Town, Albuquerque, New Mexico: A Guide to Its History and Architecture*. Special Collections, Albuquerque/Bernalillo County Library.

Vinegar, Tom. *A Walk Around Old Town*. Albuquerque, NM: Vinegar Tom Press, 1970. Special Collections, Albuquerque/Bernalillo County Library.

Charles Mann Barn and Store

Albuquerque Citizen, December 9, 1908. Chronicling America, Library of Congress.

Albuquerque Evening Citizen, October 30, 1906. Chronicling America, Library of Congress.

Carlson, Paul, and Geraldine Snow. "A Genealogical Walking Tour of Old Town." Albuquerque Museum, presented for the New Mexico Genealogical Society, October 17, 1987.

Dewitt, Susan. *Historic Albuquerque Today: An Overview Survey of Historic Buildings and Districts*. 2nd ed. A publication of the Historic Landmarks Survey of Albuquerque. Albuquerque, NM, September 1978.

Emmer, Regina. SAH Archipedia. "Basket Shop (Florencio Zamora Store; Charles Mann Store)." sah-archipedia.org/buildings/NM-01-001-0111-06.

Fisher, Irene. "Old Albuquerque Past Present." Old Albuquerque Historical Society. Special Collections, Albuquerque/Bernalillo County Library.

Jaramillo, Prospero. "Los Ancianos Hablan: Memorias of Old Town, La Herencia del Norte." Summer 1999. Special Collections, Albuquerque/Bernalillo County Library.

Vinegar, Tom. *A Walk Around Old Town*. Albuquerque, NM: Vinegar Tom Press, 1970. Special Collections, Albuquerque/Bernalillo County Library.

Antonio Vigil House

Albuquerque Citizen, October 23, 1908, 5. Library of Congress.

Albuquerque Morning Journal, November 14, 1882, image 2. Library of Congress.

American History and Genealogy Project. *History of New Mexico: Its Resources and People*. Vol. 2. Pacific States Publishing Co., 1907. nmahgp. genealogyvillage.com.

Baxter, John. "Salvador Armijo, Citizen of Albuquerque 1823–1879." *New Mexico Historical Review* 53, no. 3. UNM Digital Repository.

Carlson, Paul, and Geraldine Snow. "A Genealogical Walking Tour of Old Town." Albuquerque Museum, presented for the New Mexico Genealogical Society, October 17, 1987.

Dewitt, Susan. *Historic Albuquerque Today: An Overview Survey of Historic Buildings and Districts*. 2nd ed. A publication of the Historic Landmarks Survey of Albuquerque. Albuquerque, NM, September 1978.

Johnson, Byron. *Old Town, Albuquerque, New Mexico: A Guide to Its History and Architecture*. Special Collections, Albuquerque/Bernalillo County Library.

Sanborn Fire Insurance Map from Albuquerque, Bernalillo County, NM, April 1931. Library of Congress Geography and Map Division, Washington, D.C.

White, James. Transcribed by C.W. Barnum, Bernalillo County Post Offices.

Wikipedia. "Antonio Vigil House." en.wikipedia.org/wiki/Antonio_Vigil_House.

Salvador Armijo House

Baxter, John. "Salvador Armijo, Citizen of Albuquerque 1823–1879." *New Mexico Historical Review* 53, no. 3. UNM Digital Repository.

Dewitt, Susan. *Historic Albuquerque Today: An Overview Survey of Historic Buildings and Districts*. 2nd ed. A publication of the Historic Landmarks Survey of Albuquerque. Albuquerque, NM, September 1978.

State of New Mexico Records Center and Archives. "Salvador Armijo House." May 7, 1976, Albuquerque, NM.

Territorial Fair

Albuquerque City Directory, 1883. R917.8961. Special Collections, Albuquerque/Bernalillo County Library, Albuquerque, New Mexico.

Albuquerque Morning Journal, September 20, 1882, image 3. Library of Congress.

Johnson, Byron. *Old Town, Albuquerque, New Mexico: A Guide to Its History and Architecture*. Special Collections, Albuquerque/Bernalillo County Library.

Minor League Baseball. "ABQ Baseball History: Isotopes." www.milb.com/albuquerque/fans/abq-baseball-history.

Stanley, F. *The Duke City: The Story of Albuquerque, New Mexico, 1706–1956*. 1963. Special Collections, Albuquerque/Bernalillo County Library.

Steele, Thomas J. *Works and Days: A History of San Felipe Neri Church, 1867–1895*. Albuquerque, NM: Albuquerque Museum, 1983.

ABOUT THE AUTHOR

Debra "Debbie" Montoya is a native of Albuquerque, growing up in the heart of Old Town Plaza from generations of the early pioneers of the "Villa de Alburquerque." Her personal passion to accomplish writing this book occurred after the death of her beloved "Nana," Linda Rambes-Garcia, from a spiritual calling. This book is dedicated to Nana for her deep love of her home, Old Town Plaza; her parish, San Felipe de Neri Church; and her patron saint, Philip Neri. The stories written in this book contain actual family knowledge told to generations in Debbie's family.

She has been an employee of the University of New Mexico for over thirty-five years and is a graduate of Albuquerque High School, class of 1984. She has served the San Felipe de Neri Parish community along with her family and two children. When she is not writing, she restores antique French provincial furniture, documents family genealogy and enjoys concerts, traveling and spending time with her family.

Linda Rambes-Garcia and Debra Montoya. *Personal collection by Debra Montoya, 2022.*

Visit us at
www.historypress.com